PASSPORT

English for International Communication

TEACHER'S GUIDE

Angela Buckingham

Oxford University Press

Oxford University Press
Great Clarendon Street, Oxford OX2 6DP

Oxford New York
Athens Auckland Bangkok Bogotá Buenos Aires
Calcutta Cape Town Chennai Dar es Salaam
Delhi Florence Hong Kong Istanbul Karachi
Kuala Lumpur Madrid Melbourne Mexico City
Mumbai Nairobi Paris São Paulo Shanghai
Singapore Taipei Tokyo Toronto Warsaw

and associated companies in
Berlin Ibadan

OXFORD and OXFORD ENGLISH
are trade marks of Oxford University Press

ISBN 0 19 451336 X

© Oxford University Press 1995

First published 1995
Fourth impression 2001

Photocopying

Printed in Hong Kong

Illustrated by
Geo Parkin
Technical Graphics Department, Oxford University Press

Designed by
Jeffrey Tabberner

Acknowledgement

The author and publisher would like to thank the U. S.
Department of Justice for their permission to reproduce
the I-94 form on page 81.

Contents

Introduction

Passport is a course in listening and speaking skills for false-beginner or elementary level Japanese students of English who are planning to go abroad for the first time. The type of student at whom this course is aimed is the learner who has studied English for a considerable length of time at high school, but who has had little opportunity to speak the language and lacks the ability to understand English as it is spoken by a native speaker. Written primarily for college students, this course should nonetheless be of use for students returning to the classroom after a long absence: the first-time business traveler, for instance, may find it of interest. The materials in this course have been written in Japan, tested on Japanese students, and aim to guide the learner through a variety of situations which the first-time visitor abroad will encounter.

Passport contains twenty units. Each unit contains enough material for 60–90 minutes of class time. There are background notes for each unit written in both English and Japanese, which can be used in a variety of ways to suit teacher and learners: the notes can be read by the students before class as preparation; they may be used during the lesson in conjunction with the class activities; or you may wish to assign these notes as follow-up material, for review after class. On the whole, though, the authors intend that the background notes be used before the lesson proper, in order to provide the necessary background knowledge (e.g., cultural, thematic, linguistic) to help the learners understand and benefit from the lesson.

The language taught in *Passport* is North American English, primarily because this is the language that students in Japan are taught at school and are most familiar with. However, it should be noted that some of the characters in *Passport* visit Australia and the U.K., and therefore these units feature British and Australian English, too. In addition, throughout the book, the background notes draw attention to international usage. On the cassette, students will encounter a variety of accents and, overall, it is the intention of the authors that the course will be of use to the international traveler, using international English.

Passport is a complete course in itself and is intended for use as the sole text for a conversation class; but it may also be used as a supplementary textbook for single-skill listening or speaking classes. It could also be used to supplement main course conversation textbooks. However, *Passport* does loosely follow the adventures of the five main characters introduced at the start of the book and the authors wrote the course assuming that the units will be taught in order.

Approach

The primary goal of *Passport* is to teach communicative competence; by the end of the course, the learners should be able to communicate in English to a reasonable degree in a variety of situations. The situations covered in *Passport* are those which were felt to be potentially the most problematic for first-time travelers abroad. Students' perceptions of the language areas they need were also solicited and taken into account. *Passport* therefore aims to teach the lexis, grammar, and functions that learners perceive as the most important for their needs.

These language areas are taught within a communicative framework, and many of the activities and exercises in the book are student-centered. Pairwork is seen as an integral part of the course, increasing the opportunities for students to speak, and providing intensive practice for real-life situations that the learners will encounter outside the classroom.

Course components

The Student Book

The Student Book has been designed from the outset with the learner in mind. The pages are uncluttered and easy to follow, in a single-column format, with the language study section, *Look and learn*, highlighted in order to draw attention to the key phrases and lexis. Each unit is intended to be student-friendly, with stimulating tasks and exercises. Sufficient guided practice is given before students try out the target language for themselves in the *Activity*: learners hear, drill, and practice the target language before producing it themselves. Each unit is geared towards achieving a particular goal, for example, being able to change money in an exchange bureau or asking for help at a bus stop. You are encouraged to utilize the list found at the start of the *Background notes* as review, to reinforce in the learners' minds that they have achieved this goal.

The cassette

The accompanying cassette contains the listening activity at the start of each unit, as well as the main dialog, *Conversation*, which is the focal point of the unit. As noted above, a number of different native-speaker accents can be heard on the cassette. The symbol ▣▣ indicates in the Student's Book that the cassette should be used with that activity.

The Teacher's Guide

This book contains easy-to-follow lesson plans for each unit, supplementary photocopiable activities and optional activities, advice and ideas for setting up these activities in class, and the tapescripts.

Unit format

The units are organized around a variety of communicative functions (e.g., going through Immigration, understanding directions), and the unit title indicates the topic area. Each unit contains five sections as follows:

Listening

The first listening section consists of a simple task-based activity such as checking the correct boxes, circling *True* or *False*, or writing short answers to questions. This introduces in context the target language of the unit, and in a non-threatening way activates students' passive knowledge. This process can be aided by using the illustration at the beginning of the unit and the ideas suggested in the warming-up activity notes in the lesson plan in the Teacher's Guide. The recordings on the cassette are scripted dialogs but incorporate hesitations and natural pauses to introduce students to these features of speech. As mentioned above, a variety of accents are heard. These listening tasks are short, simple, and relevant, aiming to increase students' confidence in their abilities.

Look and learn

This is the language study section of each unit and sets out the target structures of the unit. These are most commonly presented as questions and answers for the students to study and then practice in pairs (e.g., the questions that a hotel receptionist is likely to ask, and possible replies). In the unit-by-unit notes, the authors suggest that you exploit fully the initial listening tasks and then drill these target structures before letting the students read through this section. This will give the students time to practice saying the words before seeing them on the page. This method bypasses pronunciation problems caused by the lack of correspondence between English spelling and English pronunciation, and promotes student confidence. The language items presented in *Look and learn* are essential, basic structures that learners will need to be able to recognize or produce on their trip abroad. New vocabulary is also introduced in this section and teachers may wish to encourage learners to record the new lexical items they encounter, and also to remind learners of the bilingual wordlist in the back of the Student's Book.

Conversation

This is the focal point of each unit, and consists of a listening task based on a conversation. The target structures from *Look and learn* are thus reinforced in a natural situational context which provides the first real opportunity for learners to try out the language. In most units, the listening task is a fill-in-the-blanks, to be completed either while listening, or speculatively beforehand and then checked as the cassette is played. While the initial listening tasks in each unit tend to activate "top-down" processing skills (students listen and use their background knowledge, the situation and context to infer meaning and complete gist and detailed listening tasks), the listening tasks in the *Conversation* section tend to require more "bottom-up" processing skills (students use their knowledge of grammatical structures and vocabulary, plus other micro-skills, to decode the conversational English heard and to complete the task). This is a simplification, of course, as an integrated listening strategy is promoted and is probably brought to bear in all listening activities.

Having completed the conversation, students practice reading and acting it out in pairs. As with the language focus above, however, the authors recommend the teacher to model and drill the conversation before the students practice it intensively.

Over to you!

As the title implies, now it is the turn of the learners to expand and build upon the conversation already studied. *Over to you!* is a basic substitution drill: students are given the prompts and invited to practice the conversation, substituting the new information. This exercise provides further controlled practice for the students and also shows how basic linguistic patterns can be manipulated. This may be an important consideration for your students, who may be used to memorizing and reciting dialogs but are often unable to manipulate language already known.

Activity

These oral exercises are intended to provide the freer practice stage of the lesson, where students can expand creatively upon the language and skills practiced in the unit. Where possible, personalization is encouraged to increase student motivation (e.g., in Unit 4, students practice reserving a hotel room and may use their own names and personal details if they wish; in Unit 10, they talk about their family to their partner).

The *Activity* usually takes the form of a role-play between two people and is intended to give the learners intensive classroom practice of a real-world situation they are likely to encounter overseas. Occasionally, class games (such as *Find someone who...* in Unit 12) are incorporated into this section, but in general, class games and optional activities have been reserved for the Teacher's Book.

Out and About units

In addition to the twenty regular units which are set out as in the outline given above, there are three *Out and About* units which show the five characters in different daily situations in the countries they are visiting. The three topic areas are *Sightseeing*, *Eating out*, and *Getting around*.

These pages can be used in a variety of ways. Here are some ideas:

- as cultural teaching spots. Bring in maps, pictures, photos, timetables, postcards, promotional videos, and any other realia on hand, with the intention of giving the students a real sense of the country they are to visit. Point out where the characters are, and draw comparisons between Japan and the country you are discussing. From the *Out and About* pages, students should be able to glean cultural information about areas ranging from clothes, shop signs, and the weather, to quirks of language and cultural behavior. It is hoped that you will use these pages as a springboard to other activities. Mother tongue discussions may be appropriate for some classes; other groups may be interested in interviewing you, the teacher, for insights into your culture and country. If your yearly schedule and teaching establishment allow for it, native speaker guests may be brought in and interviewed about their country. Tourist offices, English newspapers, international television and radio broadcasts are all good sources of authentic material and information to help you bring real life into the classroom. For example, in *Out and About 1 (Sightseeing)*, Rie and Miki are seen in front of the Golden Gate Bridge. This provides an opportunity for you to elicit information about the San Francisco area and to provide any information required. In *Out and About 2 (Eating out)*, Makoto and Mayumi are seen having lunch in a British pub garden, opening the way for a class brainstorm on food in different countries and where we eat it. This approach is fairly limitless; and the teacher's notes relating to each unit provide some more ideas you may wish to use.

- as further role-play practice. The students pretend to be the characters on the page and act out the cartoon dialogs given. More advanced groups can substitute information and even add to the conversation as their language skills allow. Encouraging learners to stand up in class and act while they speak encourages the learners to see the language as a means for communication rather than as an object of study; it can also aid memorization for some students and some students will enjoy the activity simply for the fun it provides as a break in class routine. However, bear in mind that some students may feel very uncomfortable with drama activities and it is clearly important to be sympathetic to learner anxieties in the group.

- as a guide for teaching appropriate behavior, and the language that is most important for good relations with the people of another country. You can, for example, focus on polite expressions (e.g., *excuse me*, *please*, *thank you*) that are a feature of the *Out and About* units. It may be useful to ask students what they would say in similar situations in Japanese, and to compare the English expressions with those they would use in Japanese.

- as a stimulus for students to design their own *Out and About* pages as wall posters. Possible topics could include shopping, greetings, hotels, weather, farewells, pubs and cafés, and so on. College students seem to be very good at project-type activities such as these, and their posters are often colorful, informative, and a good learning resource. Put finished posters on the wall and let the class look at them (and explain them if language ability allows). The posters can be added to as new phrases and useful expressions are encountered in class.

- as material for memorization or drills, particularly of formulaic language, e.g., *Here you are*, *Thanks a lot*. Learners need to be able to produce such language automatically in order to function smoothly in the foreign country.

Lesson planning

It is important to plan a lesson for each class that you teach. This ensures that you are fully prepared for the class, and are aware of your goals and teaching objectives before the lesson starts. This Teacher's Book gives possible lesson plans which you may wish to utilize, but remember that you might need to adapt and alter these outline plans according to the level and the needs of your particular students. Bear in mind that individual learning styles differ and that you should always try to incorporate a variety of activities into your lessons. The outline lesson plans that are found here should enable you to produce lessons which are organized and comprehensive, and which enable your students to learn and produce the target structures in the book.

Using the Teacher's Guide

The lesson plans in this book are explained under the following headings:

Review

Begin each lesson with a review of the previous class. This helps to consolidate material already taught, enables you to assess how well the students are coping and how much is really being absorbed, and starts the lesson in a positive way (the students are not learning anything new and their ability to produce English should boost their confidence). It also helps to remind students of the importance of regular review: some may have very poor study habits and need all the help they can get in this regard. Review activities should be exciting, fun, and confidence-boosting: the ideas in this book include games, quizzes, and role-plays.

Warming up

This section gives suggestions for starting the lesson proper. Warming-up activities help to activate students' passive knowledge of the topic area and prepare them to start the class. This section gives ideas for appropriate realia you may wish to bring into class, vocabulary you may need to pre-teach, and activities to help your lesson get off to a good start. This section also reminds teachers to use the bilingual *Background notes* as a valuable teaching resource.

Open your books

This takes you step-by-step through the lesson, giving detailed suggestions on how to set up activities and possible student problems that you may encounter. The notes explain how to present the target structures, give controlled practice of the language, and lead the students to thoroughly practice and internalize the material before they are expected to produce it. Optional activities are found throughout this section. You may wish to use them to supplement the basic lesson plan, according to the level and the needs of your group.

Finishing the lesson

This section explains how to bring together all the material taught in the lesson and to consolidate in the learners' minds what they have studied in the class. This acts as a basic review and clarifies to the students the key points of the lesson. It also enables the lesson to end, as it started, on a positive note, as students are reminded of the new things they have learned and the uses to which they can be put. Extension activities, such as games and homework tasks, can also be found here.

Time guidelines

The timing of lessons is often the biggest problem area for teachers. Before you start using *Passport*, calculate how much time you will be spending with your students over a week, a month, and the academic year. Try to ascertain how much time you will be able to spend on review, and whether outside factors (public holidays, examination schedules, etc.) will affect your class schedule. The length of class will, of course, vary from institution to institution, but here are some possible outlines for teaching a complete unit in one lesson:

50-minute lesson

5 minutes	*Review* of material taught in the previous lesson.
5 minutes	*Warming up* using *Background notes*, realia; pre-teach new lexis as necessary.
35 minutes	*Open your books*
5 minutes	*Finishing the lesson*: rounding-off activities, consolidation and review.

90-minute lesson

10 minutes	*Review* of material taught in the previous lesson.
10 minutes	*Warming up* using *Background notes*, realia; pre-teach new lexis as necessary.
60 minutes	*Open your books*
10 minutes	*Finishing the lesson*: rounding-off activities, consolidation and review.

However, this outline will push the learners through the material at quite a fast pace, and you may find that it is worth spending longer in class on fewer activities in the Student Book unit. As supplementary material, you can use some of the optional activities found in the lesson plans in this Teacher's Guide, and refer to the bilingual *Background notes* in class. If you decide to adopt this approach, it may not be feasible to cover a whole unit in one lesson, and you may wish to follow an outline such as this:

Lesson 1	**Lesson 2**
Review	Warming up
Warming up	Review *Look and learn*
Listening	*Conversation*
Optional activities	*Over to you!*
Look and learn	Optional activities
Optional activities	*Activity*
Finishing the lesson	Finishing the lesson

Passport is an extremely flexible textbook, and it is up to you, the teacher, to decide how best to utilize it for the learners in your classes.

Before you start
Preliminary activities for the first lesson

Warming up

Since this is your first lesson with the group, aim to spend as much time as you can afford in getting to know the students in your class before you start on the book. Name-learning games, introduction activities, setting up any class rules you feel are important, and so on, can all occur before the first proper lesson.

These valuable class-gelling activities are always worth spending some time on. Invite the class to ask you questions, too, and try to gauge the class level and atmosphere. Remember that if this is the class's first time with a native speaker teacher, some students will be feeling understandably nervous, and it would be wise for you as a teacher to help them relax and get ready to enjoy speaking English. Try not to say too much yourself and scare your students! Be friendly, calm, and reassuring. Find out if any of the group has traveled abroad, where to, and if they spoke English at all when they were there.

If you speak Japanese, you may wish to hold a class discussion in the mother tongue to assess the students' attitudes to English: Why are the class here? Are they planning to travel, or is this class compulsory for them? Are they highly motivated, or will you need to create interest to motivate them? On the other hand, try not to judge your students too quickly. This is, after all, only the first class and some groups take longer than others to warm up!

Passport has been written on the assumption that your students will be going overseas after completing the book. Find out if your students are planning any trips abroad and where they're hoping to go. This will give you some advance warning to collect as much realia (maps, brochures, posters, etc.) as you can beforehand to use throughout the course. Travel agencies and tourist promotion offices are good sources for these kinds of item. Take your time with the first few lessons to set the tone for the rest of the course; you want your learners to enjoy the experience of studying English with you, so it's worth getting it right!

Optional Activities: Name-learning games
Beanbag throws

Take in a small beanbag or ball. Students sit in a circle. Give a student the beanbag and gesture for him/her to throw it to you. When you catch the ball, say clearly: *My name's… What's your name?* As you ask the question, make eye contact with a confident-looking student and throw the beanbag to him/her. They should continue the drill.

If they don't pick it up right away, indicate that the beanbag should be thrown back to you, so that you can repeat the words as necessary until everyone understands. Repeat around the circle randomly until everyone has said their name. If you want to take it a stage further, the drill can be continued but the thrower has to make eye contact and say: *Your name's…* to the person who catches the beanbag. If they get the name right, the catcher stands up. Continue until everyone in the circle is standing up (i.e., everyone has been named). This can be a hilarious game if you can encourage the students to speed up the throwing, and it's a great way to learn names quickly.

Sticky labels

(More able students only, as this activity requires the ability to make spontaneous mini-conversations. As it is your first class, use your discretion as to whether or not they will be able to cope!)

Hand out a sticky label to all the students. Tell them to write their name in the top left-hand corner, their favorite musicians in the top right-hand corner, a sport they like in the bottom left-hand corner, and something they hate in the bottom right-hand corner. They then stick their labels on their chests, and walk around talking to each other about what they have written. You may prefer to write up some sample mini-dialogs on the board, e.g.:

> A: *Hi! My name's Keiko.*
> B: *Nice to meet you, Keiko. I'm Kenichi.*
> A: *So, you like skiing?*
> B: *Yes, that's right. I love it! How about you?*
> A: *I like tennis, actually. But I like skiing, too!*

Meanwhile, you should take notes about the students. After everyone has talked to at least five other people, bring the class back together and ask some questions based on the notes you have made, e.g.:

> *Who is Keiko?*
> *Who hates enka?*
> *Who likes scuba-diving?*

This reinforces to students the importance of actually listening to each other when having conversations in English, and is a fun way to find out early on what hobbies and interests the learners in the group have.

A way of adapting this game is to turn it into a questioning activity (again, quite demanding for false-beginner level students). Instead of writing their notes on labels, they use scrap paper, which you collect in and redistribute. Students then question the people they meet in order to find the person who wrote the paper they have been given, e.g.:

> A: *Is your name Keiko?*
> B: *No, it isn't. I'm Junko. Do you like skiing?*
> A: *Yes, I do. But my favorite sport is volleyball.*

Conduct feedback as in the original activity.

Name chain game

Students sit in a circle. Set up a clapping rhythm (e.g., students slap their legs, clap their hands, and then click their fingers: slap, clap, click! slap, clap, click!) Students speak in turn around the circle, keeping in time with the rhythm set up, e.g.:

Student 1

slap	clap	click!	slap	clap	click!
My	*name's*	*Sanae,*	*and I*	*like*	*skiing.*

Student 2

slap	clap	click!	slap	clap	click!
Your	*name's*	*Sanae,*	*and you*	*like*	*skiing.*
My	*name's*	*Kenichi,*	*and I*	*like*	*rock music.*

This proceeds around the circle. This activity is probably best played in small groups of about six or seven students. At the end of the game, ask the students to try to remember everyone's name and what their hobbies are. Open this up into a class feedback session so that everyone learns everybody else's names.

Introducing pairwork

Students who are not used to studying in the communicative classroom may also need some introduction to the notion of pairwork. Every unit in *Passport* requires that students are comfortable working together in pairs, using only English when they do so, without reverting to the mother tongue. For false-beginner level students studying in a monolingual group, often in large classes, this can be a very demanding situation and the temptation to revert to Japanese to complete a task can be high. From your very first class, encourage your students to use only English where possible. If possible, in your first lessons, hold mother tongue discussions to explain the reasoning behind this, or more simply, use positive reinforcement and congratulate students who do make the effort to communicate in English.

Pairwork procedure is probably best explained early on. Students should turn their chair so that they face their partner, make eye contact with their partner when speaking, ask for repetition when they don't understand, not look at their partner's book when completing an information-gap activity, and so on.

Teach your students "emergency language" and encourage them to use it (e.g., *I'm sorry, I don't understand. I'm sorry, could you say that again please?*).

Consider the advantages of different ways of pairing in your classroom (e.g., strong with weak student; male with female; friends; students of similar ability; with the person sitting next to them; with someone they don't usually sit next to). Try to use all these types at different times in your lessons.

Optional Activity

Introduction to pairwork: "What's your name?" game

Write this chart on the board and tell students to copy it onto a piece of paper.

	me	Student 1	Student 2	Student 3	Student 4
Name					
Hometown					
Birthday					
Hobby					

Drill the questions and answers:

What's your name?	*My name's …*
Where are you from?	*I'm from …*
When's your birthday?	*It's in …*

(Check that everyone knows the months of the year!)

What's your hobby?	*I like …*

Give the students a few minutes to write short answers about themselves in the *me* column. Then ask them to interview four people they don't know in the class and to note down their answers. Set up three rules:

1 No Japanese may be used.

2 Students must make eye contact when they speak.

3 Students must not look at their partner's paper.

Give the students 10–15 minutes to conduct their interviews. At the end of the activity, congratulate those students who kept to all three rules, and ask some general feedback questions (e.g., *Who is this? What's her hobby?*).

This is a very simple introduction to pairwork. Students very quickly become used to the idea that pairwork constitutes an important part of each lesson as it keeps recurring!

Depending upon the seating arrangements in your classroom, you may need to ask students to turn their chairs or desks to face each other during pairwork stages of the lesson. Again, this is very often a departure from normal classroom procedures, so train your learners to move furniture quickly, quietly, and efficiently so that activities can be set up with the minimum of fuss.

Once you have established class rules and learner goals, learned names, and held any other preliminary activities you wish to, it is time to begin using the book.

Spend a few minutes asking the students to look at *Passport* and to become familiar with the format. Point out the *Background notes* and the bilingual wordlist at the back of the book and explain how you wish the students to use them. Before the students study a unit in class, they should read through the *Background notes* for that unit as homework. Show the students the contents list and, if you wish, explain the rate at which you'll be moving through the twenty units. (This will depend upon the number of lessons you have with the class over how long a period of time.) Tell the students what they will need to bring to your lesson each time (e.g., notebook or file, a vocabulary book, a dictionary). If you won't be using the book in your first class, assign the *Background notes* for the first unit as homework for the class to read before the next lesson.

Introducing the five characters

Optional Activity

Discussion:
Traveling abroad – What's the best way?

Ask your class who has been abroad. If some students have, ask how they traveled, which airline they used, if they used a travel agency to organize their hotels, and other similar questions. If no one has been overseas, ask which countries they would most like to visit.

At some point, turn the questioning around to the subject of cost. See if the students know how much package tours cost and brainstorm advantages and disadvantages of going on an organized trip. (Some possible answers: good points – easy to make new friends, no worries about accommodation, everything done for you; bad points – expensive, difficult to meet local people, little freedom to go where you want to go.)

Tell the class that in this book they will meet five Japanese characters: Miki, Rie, Koji, Mayumi, and Makoto, who are traveling overseas to three different countries. Bring in a world map if you have one to show where each character is going. Tell the students that they are going to read about these five people.

Students read through the introductions to the five characters on p. 5 of their books. This could be done in several ways:

Jigsaw reading
Put students into small groups. In a class of 18, for example, make six groups of three. Students call themselves A, B, or C in their group. Tell two groups to read through the information about Miki and Rie, two groups to read about Koji, and two groups to read about Mayumi and Makoto. When they have finished,

regroup the students so that there are three groups, A, B, and C. The new groups thus consist of students who know about each character. With their books closed, students tell their new group members about the character they read about. For weaker classes, you may wish to put some general questions up on the board for the students to try to answer, e.g.:

> *Which country are Miki and Rie / Koji / Mayumi and Makoto visiting?*
>
> *What are Miki's hobbies? How about Rie?*
>
> *Has Miki been overseas before? How about Rie?*
>
> *Which place does Rie really want to visit?*
>
> *How old is Koji?*
>
> *What does he like doing?*
>
> *What will he do in Sydney?*
>
> *What is Mayumi's favorite movie?*
>
> *What does Makoto worry about?*

Comprehension questions
If jigsaw reading is too advanced an activity for your class, ask students to read through the introductions in pairs, helping each other with the meaning where necessary. Remind learners of the wordlist at the back of the book. When they have finished, have them close their books and ask some of the questions listed above.

Student feedback
An alternative way to conduct feedback after the page has been read through is to write the names of the characters on the board, and ask students to write anything they can remember about the characters under the appropriate name. This is a fun task, especially if your class is small enough to make it into a kind of team competition (*Who can remember most?*).

When you have finished introducing the five characters, tell the class that they are found in every unit and so they will get used to hearing American, Australian, and British English voices on the cassette, even though the book is written in American English.

Unit 1
Would you like beef or fish?

Topic / functions

Asking for things politely

Accepting and refusing things politely

Asking for repetition

Review

Clearly, no review is possible to any great extent in the first lesson, but if you have followed the suggestions made in the *Preliminary Activities* unit, you should see if your students can remember any information about the five characters introduced on p. 5 and remind students about any "emergency language" they learned in the first lesson.

Ask the students to work in pairs. Write the names Koji, Mayumi, Makoto, Rie, and Miki on the board. Give the students a few minutes to try to remember as much information as they can about the characters. Ask: *Who are these people? Where are they going? What are their hobbies? What do you remember about them? Tell your partner four things about each person. What can you remember?*

Give examples if necessary, demonstrating the pairwork with another student. After a few minutes, nominate some students to tell you what they could remember.

Warming up

Preview: Background notes for Unit 1

Ask the students if they read the *Background notes*. If you like, give the students a few minutes, in pairs, to discuss in Japanese what they read. If you prefer not to have the students speak Japanese in class, ask some general questions about the notes. Higher-level classes may be able to tell you what happens during the flight, which form you have to fill out, what kind of duty-free goods you can buy, etc. If you didn't ask the students to look at these notes before the lesson, ask them to do so for homework after your first class. Put the list of functions at the top of this page on the board and tell the students that they will learn how to do these things in this, the first class.

Optional Activity

Scrambled words

Put a list of scrambled vocabulary on the board and do the first one as an example. Ask the students to work in pairs to unscramble the words. The first pair to finish is the winner! For example: Food and drink and things you'll need on the plane

offeec	*coffee*
ate	*tea*
reeb	*beer*
blkenat	(*a*) *blanket*
illpow	(*a*) *pillow*
spawenrep	(*a*) *newspaper*

When putting new vocabulary on the board for Japanese students, it is good to get into the habit of always using the article (*a* or *the*). This will help to remind your students to use the article.

Open your books

Tell the students to look at the picture of Koji on p. 6. Ask questions to elicit useful vocabulary related to flying. Read the caption aloud: *Koji is on a flight to Sydney. He is deciding what to eat.*

Ask: *What is the woman's job? What is she holding? What kinds of drinks can you see? What is this?* (point to the pillow, blanket, headset, etc.).

Teach any unknown vocabulary and write it on the board (see the note above about recording new lexis). If your students use vocabulary books, ask them to write down the new words.

Listening

Read the instructions aloud clearly, then read through the sentences one at a time so that students understand the sentences before listening to the cassette. Mime *blanket* and *pillow* so that everyone is clear about the meaning of these words. When everyone is ready, play the cassette and monitor unobtrusively to check that everyone understands and is completing the task. With less confident classes, you may wish to stop the tape after the first dialogue and ask students to check their answers together, to reassure each other that they have understood what to do.

After playing the cassette through once, tell the students to check their answers together in pairs. Say: *Work in pairs. Check your answers together. Do you have the same answers?*

Play the cassette again, this time stopping after each dialog to give the students time to understand more fully the conversation they hear. If students are struggling, replay the key sentences (e.g., *Apple juice, please!*) and pause after playing them.

Tell students to check their answers again in pairs. This important stage gives the students a chance to get feedback from each other, and change their answers if they wish, before you ask for answers in front of the class.

Nominate students to tell you the answers. Write them on the board. If necessary, play the dialogues one more time, pointing to the answers as they occur.

Answers:
1 some apple juice
2 beef
3 coffee
4 a pillow
5 an English newspaper

Optional Activity

Using the tapescript
Using the tapescript frequently is not recommended, as it tends to make students try to understand every word, whereas at this level they need training in skills such as gist listening, prediction, and understanding inferences. However, occasionally you may wish to use the tapescript for additional practice, or for teaching points such as intonation patterns.

In this unit, Japanese students tend to have problems with the use of *or*, as in *Would you like tea or coffee?* / *We have beef or fish*. Hand out the tapescript and ask students to highlight the key points you wish to focus on. Replay the tape and draw intonation arrows on the board above the words, to show that the flight attendant is offering one or the other. Act out holding a pot of tea and a pot of coffee, and indicate that students can choose one or the other, not both!

Higher-level students can practice reading the tapescript through in pairs and acting out the conversations, although this is probably better left to a later stage in the lesson.

Look and learn

Books closed. Model the sentences clearly but at normal speed and with natural intonation. Drill the questions and answers in chorus, and when students are confident, nominate individuals to repeat the sentences after you. Be diligent about correcting pronunciation and work on any difficult sounds or words, such as *Would you, Could you,* and (*Here*) *you are.*

Concentrate especially on the emergency language: *I'm sorry, I don't understand.* / *Sorry. Could you repeat that, please?* / *Could you say that more slowly, please?* Make a mental note to encourage students to use these phrases throughout the course.

When everyone has practiced all the sentences, say: *Open your books at page 6. Look at the questions and answers. Practice in pairs.*

The key to success in this section is repetition, as

students need time to absorb and internalize the target language. Don't rush the class through the *Look and learn* section but instead encourage students to repeat the questions and answers several times (not just once!). If your class dislikes practicing, have them change partners several times to encourage recycling. Tell more able students to close their books halfway through the practice phase to see if they can ask and answer without reading the sentences.

Optional Activities

Realia drill
Bring in an English language newspaper, a Japanese newspaper, a blanket, a pillow, and any other items that could be used in the drill. Hold up the blanket and say: *Ask me: blanket* to a student to elicit: *I'd like a blanket, please.* If the student doesn't catch on, feed the sentence to him/her. When everyone understands, go through each of the items in turn.

If your class is small (20 students or fewer), ask them to sit in a circle and set up a chaining drill, where one person in each pair is given an object as a prompt. After making a question and answer in their pairs, shout *Change!*, whereupon the object is passed to the next pair in the circle and the process is repeated.

Emergency language posters
Hand out large sheets of colored paper and tell students to design posters that will help them remember useful emergency language. Elicit or teach useful questions and phrases, and write them up on the board, e.g.:

Excuse me, can you help me?

I'm sorry, I don't understand.

Could you repeat that, please?

Could you say that again, please?

Could you say that more slowly, please?

Pardon me?

The posters could include as many sentences as possible, or just one phrase. Encourage the students to work quickly (you may wish to ban the use of erasers to speed things up a bit!) or ask them to finish the posters for homework. Display the posters on the wall around the classroom and use them regularly!

Conversation

Hold your Student's book so the students can see p. 7. Say: *Look at page 7. Look at the "Conversation."* Read the instructions aloud and check that everyone knows what to do. Play the cassette and, if necessary, stop after the first question and elicit the answer. Then play the rest of the conversation without stopping.

After playing the cassette through once, tell the students to check their answers together. Say: *Work in pairs. Check your answers together. Do you have the same answers?*

Say: *Now listen again.* Play the cassette again, this

time stopping after each blank in the book to give the students time to check their answers. If necessary, play the tape a third time.

After letting the students check their answers again in pairs, check the answers as a class. You may wish to write the whole conversation on the board and ask different students to fill in the blanks; or you may just wish to nominate different students to tell you the answers. Write the answers on the board to let everyone check their spelling.

Answers:
1 chicken or fish
2 fish
3 some wine
4 some wine
5 a beer

Books closed. Model the conversation or use the cassette, drilling chorally. Concentrate upon natural intonation. Model the stress on *Certainly*. If possible, act out with appropriate gestures and facial expressions (*Here you are, I don't understand,* etc.) to make the meaning as clear as possible for the lowest-level learners in the class. After sufficient drilling, tell the students to look again at p. 7 and to practice the conversation in pairs.

Optional Activity

"Read, look up, and speak" technique
As it is very unnatural to have students read aloud in class, encourage learners to act out their conversations in as natural a way as possible. One way to do this is to tell students that they can read the sentences, but when they speak they must look up from the page and make eye contact with their partner. This is best set up by example: pretend to be a student and work with a partner in this way. Exaggerating what you are doing makes this clear! This is a very useful technique which helps wean students away from their dependence on the written word.

Confident classes can start to role-play the conversation, acting out the part of the flight attendant and passenger and miming giving and receiving items.

Over to you!

This is a basic substitution drill. Put students in new pairs. Say: *Now practice the conversation again. Look at "Over to you!" Make four new conversations, using this information.*

You may need to do an example with a student to make this clear the first time. Monitor the activity unobtrusively and listen out for any pronunciation problems. Remind students to make eye contact when they speak. You may need to model *lamb* (silent *b*) for weaker students.

If students are becoming monotonal as they read, stop

the activity and re-model the correct intonation. As with the *Look and learn* section, encourage students to practice each conversation several times, until they can do it automatically, only glancing down at the page occasionally.

Listen out for errors in the use of the article. Some students may start producing sentences such as: **I'd like a fish. / *I'd like a some coffee.* Correct these before they become an ingrained habit.

Optional Activity

Conversation prompts
After practicing the conversation several times, stronger classes should be able to use the drill prompts as cues for practicing the conversation alone. Tell students to cover the conversation (but let them look occasionally!) and use the prompts alone to reconstruct the dialogue. This is quite a demanding task so ensure that the conversation has been thoroughly practiced before moving on to this stage!

Activity

New partners. Say: *Cover the words,* and gesture to show that the conversation and the prompts in *Over to you!* should be unseen. Read the instructions aloud. Put students in pairs and tell all Student As, and then Bs, to raise their hands. (This ensures that students are clear as to which role they are to play.) Say: *Look at the pictures. Student A, you are a flight attendant. Offer things to Student B* (gesture to explain offer). *Student B, you are flying to the U.S.* (or any other English-speaking country). *Accept and refuse things. Ask Student A to repeat things. Look at the pictures. Use these pictures in your conversation. Start now!*

This type of activity is very demanding for false-beginner level students, so be prepared for a few moments' silence and bewildered stares. Respond to this by smiling and gesturing to the page, and if necessary feed an opening line to the flight attendants, e.g., *Good afternoon, sir. Would you like… ?* Once a few students have caught on, you can retreat to monitor the activity and note any areas where confusion is still evident.

Halfway through the activity, ask students to change roles so that both questioning and answering are practiced. If your group is really struggling, let them look back at *Look and learn* on p. 6 for a few minutes. However, it is probably best to let them try it out as best they can, this being the most realistic stage of the lesson and the best indication of how well they are likely to cope on the flight.

When the activity winds down naturally, congratulate the class and tell them to return to their seats.

On the board, write some of the most common errors you heard, and say: *Here are some of the mistakes I heard. Can you correct them?*

Give the students a few minutes, then elicit the answers and correct the mistakes.

Optional Activity

On the plane: class role-play
To turn the activity into a full-scale role-play, bring in as much realia as possible as suggested in the realia drill on p. 13, and move chairs, desks, etc. to set the room up to resemble part of a plane (or planes, depending upon the size of your group).

Choose about a quarter of the class to role-play flight attendants; the rest are passengers. It is probably best to allocate the flight attendant roles to the stronger students in the groups. You may wish to play a part yourself for a few minutes to get the activity started. Encourage the passengers to ask as much as possible (dropping a few hints works well: *Do you want something to read? Ask him: newspaper*). You could even make a few "Captain's announcements" for classes that are participating well!

Finishing the lesson

Bring the class back together and tell students to return to their places. Congratulate those who made their best effort in the *Activity* stage of the lesson. Slow down the pace of the lesson. If you have a very confident group you can ask if there are any problems or questions the students want to ask.

Tell students to look at the *Background notes* for Unit 1. List the functions on the board and elicit an example for each one. Write the examples too, e.g.:

Asking for things politely:
May I have a glass of water, please?
Accepting things politely:
Thank you very much.
Refusing things politely:
No thank you.
Asking for repetition:
Sorry. Could you repeat that, please?

Tell the students to copy down the examples. Assign any review homework you feel is necessary (e.g., review the *Look and learn* section / write a short conversation between a flight attendant and yourself on a flight to. . . / learn the emergency language taught in the lesson).

Ask the class what happens when you land at an airport. Ask: *What do you do first? Where do you go?* Elicit or tell the class that after landing, you must go through Immigration and Customs. Tell the class that in the next lesson, they will learn how to go through Immigration and answer questions in English.

Tell the class to read the *Background notes* for Unit 2 before the next class.

Optional Activity

Review: match the sentences
Write these questions and answers on the board. Tell students to match them by drawing a line, and then practice asking and answering in pairs.

The questions:

1 Would you like chicken or fish, ma'am?
2 I'd like a pillow, please.
3 Could I have tea, please?
4 Did you see the menu?
5 What would you like to drink, sir?

The answers:

a Menu? I'm sorry, I don't understand.
b Certainly. Would you like milk and sugar?
c Of course, sir. Here you are.
d I'd like some red wine, please.
e I'd like fish, please.

Answers: 1 e 2 c 3 b 4 a 5 d

Unit 2
Can I have your passport, please?

Topic / functions

Understanding questions at Immigration

Answering questions at Immigration

Giving information about yourself

Review

Asking for things on the plane

Put the students in groups of three. Make one copy of photocopiable page A (p. 80) for each group and cut them up. Give one set of pictures to each group.

Students take turns picking up a picture and making a question about it. For example: Student picks up the picture of a glass of wine, and asks the student on the left: *Would you like some wine?*

The second student replies as he/she likes, and then picks up a new card. The process is repeated around the group until all the pictures have been used. If the group has difficulties, tell them to look back at *Look and learn* on p. 6 of their books. This is a basic drill using pictures as prompts. Monitoring the activity will give you an indication of how much language the students have retained from the previous class. Allowing the students to look back at *Look and learn* instills good study habits and reminds the learners where they can best find help when they run into problems.

Warming up

Preview: Background notes for Unit 2

Books closed. Write *Immigration* on the board and draw a stick picture to represent an immigration officer questioning a person at the airport. Ask students to tell you what kinds of things the officer will ask about. Do not expect complete questions. However, students should be able to respond with one word or short answers (e.g., *passport*, *how long*). You may wish to put some of these words in a speech bubble for the officer.

Elicit from students, or remind them, that they will have to show their passport and immigration form to the officer. If you have any real immigration forms, boarding or landing cards, visas, etc., bring them in to show to the class. Students who have not yet traveled

overseas are often interested to see this kind of realia, and the items can be used for pre-teaching useful lexical items. Ask if any students have traveled abroad and what questions they were asked at Immigration. Ask: *Was the immigration officer friendly?* Tell the class that in this unit, Miki and Rie have arrived in the U.S. and go through Immigration.

Open your books

Tell the students to look at the picture of Miki on p. 8. Read the caption aloud: *Miki is answering questions at Immigration.*

Listening

Read the instructions aloud clearly and check that everyone understands *true* and *false*. (If there is confusion, say to a student: *Your name is … True? Yes, it's true.* Repeat several times with different people, and then get some names wrong. When the student says *No!*, reply *Ah, that's false.*)

Repeat the instructions if necessary and then read through the sentences one at a time. When everyone is ready, play the tape. With less confident classes, you may wish to stop the tape after the first dialog to check that everyone understands the task and to let the students check their answers together.

After playing the cassette through once, have the class check their answers in pairs. Say: *Work in pairs. Check your answers together. Do you have the same answers?*

Say: *Now listen again.* Play the cassette again, this time stopping after each question to give the students time to understand and absorb the language heard. If the group is struggling, replay key sentences (e.g., *That's your I-94*) and pause after playing them.

Tell the students to check their answers again in pairs, before asking them to give their answers in front of the class. Play the tape one more time, stopping at the end of each dialog. Take a class vote on whether the answers are true or false. If the entire class chooses the wrong answer, play the key part of the dialog again.

Go through each dialog and write the answers on the board.

If students are worried by the last question and had trouble understanding amounts, reassure them that this area is covered in the next unit.

Answers:

1 T **2** F **3** T **4** T **5** F **6** T **7** F **8** F

Optional Activity

Why was it false?: using the tapescript

Higher-level classes may be able to tell you why an answer was false (e.g., *It's an I-94, not an I-49 form.*), but you should not expect most students at this level to be able to explain their answers. If you decide to use the tapescript after completing the task, bear in mind the comments made in the *Optional Activity* on p. 13 *(Using the tapescript).*

In these dialogs, focus upon the recycling of emergency language. Rie is weaker at English than her friend Miki, and this is reflected in the language she uses: *Excuse me? Sorry, I don't understand. Sorry, could you repeat that, please?* Use the tape to drill the correct intonation of these phrases.

Look and learn

Books closed. Model the sentences clearly but at normal speed and with natural intonation. Drill the questions and answers chorally, gesturing for students to repeat after you.

> T: *Can I have your passport, please?*
> SS: *Can I have your passport, please?*
> T: *Yes. Here you are.*
> SS: *Yes. Here you are.*

After each question and answer set, change the drill so that students respond:

> T: *Can I have your passport, please? Reply!*
> SS: *Yes. Here you are.*

When the class is ready, switch to open-pair drilling:

> T: *Junko, ask Koji: passport.*
> Junko: *Can I have your passport, please?*
> Koji: *Yes. Here you are.*

Tell the class that *What's the purpose of your visit?* and *Business or pleasure?* mean **Why** *are you here?*; and that *occupation* means *job.*

Repeat the process with the whole language study. When everyone has practiced all the sentences, tell the students: *Open your books to p. 8. Look at the questions and answers. Practice in pairs.*

Ensure that the students thoroughly practice and internalize the target structures before moving on to the next section in the unit. Change partners if necessary to provide sufficient practice, and monitor for pronunciation errors caused by reading the words. Some learners will struggle with *business* and produce *busy-ness.* The *v* sound in *vacation* is a difficult sound for Japanese students, and the word stress in *occupation* may cause problems. Give the students time to practice.

Optional Activity

Where are you going?

If your students are preparing for a real trip abroad, ask them to practice the questions and answers again, substituting their own names and real information about their trip. If they are not, ask them to practice again, using any of the information you write on the board to change some of their answers.

Write on the board randomly:

> I'm on an exchange program.
> $1,500
> £700
> I'm visiting some friends.
> With a homestay family.
> For a month.
> At the college dormitory.
> For one and a half weeks.
> I'm a college student.
> I work in a bank.

Explain any new vocabulary. Put the students in new pairs and have them practice the *Look and learn* section again using any of the new information.

Conversation

Hold your book so the students can see p. 9. Say: *Look at page 9. Look at the "Conversation."* Read the instructions aloud and check that everyone understands that this time, they have to put the answers provided into the conversation.

With weaker groups, since this is the first occurrence of this type of exercise, you may wish to do the first item as an example on the board. More able students should be able to complete the task by themselves, but have weaker groups work in pairs or groups of three to complete the task.

Read through the conversation first and explain that *intending* means *planning* and is a polite way to ask: *How long will you stay?* Give the students several minutes to complete the conversation and, if necessary, let them check their answers together in pairs before listening to the tape.

Say: *Now listen. Check your answers. Did you get it right?* Play the cassette through once and have the students check together.

Say: *Now listen again.* Replay the cassette, pausing after each blank so that students have time to change their answers if they wish. If necessary, play the cassette one more time without stopping.

Check the answers as a class. You may wish to write the whole conversation on the board and ask different students to fill in the blanks; or you may just wish to nominate students to tell you the answers.

Answers:
1 b **2** d **3** a **4** e **5** c

Books closed. Model the conversation, or use the cassette, drilling chorally. After sufficient practice, tell the students to practice the conversation in pairs, using the "read, look up and speak" technique described on p. 14. Confident groups can start to act out the conversation, standing up and handing over imaginary passports, etc.

Optional Activity

Emotional role-play

Classes that enjoy acting out the conversation can be encouraged to develop their drama skills with this simple role-play. Make cards with the following roles and give one to each student:

The immigration officer
You are very tired and angry. You hate your job, and you don't want to talk to another passenger! Ask the questions, but don't be polite!

The immigration officer
You love your job, and you have visited Japan. You love Japanese people and are very, very friendly to Japanese passengers!

The passenger
This is your first visit to the U.S. You are very nervous and shy, and you don't understand much English. Ask the immigration officer to repeat the questions.

The passenger
This is your first visit to the U.S., and you are very excited! Smile and be very friendly to the immigration officer.

Put students in pairs and ask them to act out the conversations. Different pairings will produce interesting conversations! Acting out the conversations in this way can be a powerful aid to learning and can also help improve students' intonation patterns. Exaggerated acting will be toned down in real life, but often students don't revert entirely to monotonal intonation patterns after acting out conversations in this way.

Let students perform their role-play in front of other students in the group. This is best done if you have several pairs performing at the same time. It can be very scary to perform in a foreign language in front of your peers. Bear in mind that some students are uncomfortable with drama activities: do not insist in these cases.

Over to you!

Say: *Now practice the "Conversation" again. Make three new conversations, using this information.* Do an example first if necessary. Monitor for any pronunciation problems. Offer help and corrections only as necessary. You may need to model the names of the hotels and hall.

Have the students practice several times, until they can do it by only glancing down at the page for an occasional prompt. Remind them to make eye contact with each other when they speak.

Optional Activities

Over to you!: a variation

If you prefer, allocate just one of the conversations for certain students to practice. Give the students time to practice their role and, if you like, hand out the emotion cards described above. After a few minutes, ask different groups to act out their conversations for other groups.

Conversation prompts

See p. 14.

Activity

Make one copy of photocopiable page B on p. 81 for each student. Go through each line in turn and complete the form using capital letters. As you do so, ask the students to complete the form with their personal information. Be especially careful with dates: the Japanese system records dates in the order month-day-year, but in many countries, and on international forms, day-month-year is more common.

After completing the form, go on to the role-play activity. New partners. Allocate A and B roles, and read the instructions aloud. Books closed. Give students time to warm up, and remember that this type of activity is very demanding for false-beginner level students. If your class is very weak, put some key words up on the board to jog the immigration officer's memory, e.g., *passport, I-94, purpose, address, how long, occupation, money.*

Monitor and listen for errors. If the "passengers" are struggling in the role-play, point to some of the emergency language posters on the walls around the room to remind them how to ask for repetition. Try to stay out of the activity, as this is the freer practice stage of the lesson and should give you an indication of how well the students have coped with the language taught in the lesson.

When the activity winds down naturally, congratulate students and ask them to return to their seats. On the board, write some of the errors you heard and ask the students to try to correct them. Give them a few minutes to complete the task. Elicit the correct answers and correct the sentences on the board.

Optional Activity

At Immigration: class role-play

Bring in as much realia as possible (students' own passports for passengers; rubber stamps, peaked caps, and so on for immigration officers). Set up the room to resemble Immigration at the airport. Allocate about one quarter of the class to play the officers. Tell the passengers to assume a new identity (some business travelers, some students on a graduation trip, a honeymoon couple, etc.). You may want to play a part yourself to get the activity started. Encourage as much English as possible to be spoken and at the end of the activity, congratulate those students who managed to refrain from speaking Japanese at all.

Finishing the lesson

Bring the class back together and tell students to return to their places. Slow down the pace of the lesson and give the students the opportunity to ask questions. Ask them look at the *Background notes* for Unit 2. List the functions on the board and elicit an example for each one. Write the examples too, e.g.:

Understanding questions at Immigration:
How long will you be staying?
Answering questions at Immigration:
I'll be here for two weeks.
Giving information about yourself:
I'm from Japan.

Have the students copy down the examples. Assign any review homework you feel is necessary. Ask the students what happens after you leave Immigration and Customs and have picked up your bags. Accept answers like *Catch a taxi into the city / Meet my friends.* Elicit if possible, or tell the class, that many people need to change some money before they can catch the airport bus. Tell the class that in the next lesson, they will learn how to change money.

Ask the class to read the *Background notes* for Unit 3 before the next class.

Optional Activity

Review: scrambled sentences

Write these scrambled questions on the board and ask students to work in pairs to decode them.

1   your please Can passport have I ?
2   occupation What's your ?
3   in do you What Japan do ?
4   staying be you will Where ?
5   I see May I-94 please your ?

Answers:

1   Can I have your passport, please?
2   What's your occupation?
3   What do you do in Japan?
4   Where will you be staying?
5   May I see your I-94, please?

Unit 3
Can I change some money here?

> ### Topic / functions
> Understanding amounts of money
> Asking about exchange rates
> Asking about commission

Review

At Immigration

Write these words on the board:

passport	money	purpose
address	the Holiday Inn	student
alone	I-94	$1,500
sightseeing	occupation	

Books closed. Tell students to work in pairs and to make a short conversation using all the words on the board. If necessary, allow them to look back briefly at *Look and learn* in Unit 2.

Conversation

Low-level learners have a very high tolerance for repetition of activities. If your class found the review activity above difficult, you may wish to replay the *Conversation* from Unit 2. Tell students to listen to Miki's conversation with the immigration officer with their books closed. Play the tape through once or twice, pausing if you wish after the immigration officer's questions.

Often a simple replaying of the tape can be a sufficient prompt for the learners. After listening, repeat the review activity to instill confidence. Do not go onto the new unit until the majority of the class feels comfortable with the exercise.

Warming up

Preview: Background notes for Unit 3

Books closed. Ask for the names of places where you can change money (bank, exchange office, bureau de change, moneychanger). Bring in realia to elicit or pre-teach *credit card, traveler's check, cash, bill, coin*. If your whole class is going overseas to one particular country, try to bring in some currency from that country. Students who will be visiting the U.S., for instance, will

be interested that U.S. bills are all the same size and color, unlike yen, and that they will need to be careful to look at the numbers when using that currency.

Higher-level classes may be able to tell you the advantages and disadvantages of different methods of payment. (Traveler's checks: safe, good rate at most banks, refundable if you keep a record of the numbers; but not usable everywhere. Cash: can be used anywhere, convenient; but if it's stolen, it's gone forever. Credit cards: easy to carry, convenient, some companies offer insurance if stolen; but not always accepted everywhere.)

The stereotype of the rich Japanese tourist abroad is worth discussing with higher-level groups. Many Japanese visitors overseas put themselves at unnecessary risk by carrying too much cash. As Japanese people do not use personal checkbooks, the idea of traveler's checks may seem somewhat alien, so take in sample traveler's checks if you can and show your students how to use them. If the level of the group is not up to this, simply tell your students not to carry a lot of cash when they travel because it's dangerous. The *Background notes* list some safeguards for students to take when they travel. Write on the board:

Remember! You pay	*by* check
	by credit card/
	with a credit card
	in cash

Tell the class that in this unit, Rie needs some U.S. dollars and visits a bank to change some money.

Open your books

Tell the students to look at the picture of Rie on p. 10. Read the caption aloud: *Rie is changing money in a bank.*

Listening

There should be few problems here as this type of exercise will be familiar from Unit 1. Read the sentences aloud, including the amounts of money, but do not drill them at this stage. Some learners may be confused by the large numbers but should be able to follow the sentences, even if at this stage they are unable to say the numbers with any confidence themselves.

Play the cassette through once. Say: *Work in pairs. Check your answers together. Do you have the same answers?*

Say: *Now listen again.* Play the cassette again, this time stopping after each question to give the students time to check their answers. If necessary, replay the key sentences (*Four thousand dollars!* etc.) and pause after playing them.

Tell the students to check together again in pairs. Play the tape one more time, and elicit the answers by writing the options on the board and taking a class vote. Erase the incorrect answers to leave the correct amounts up for students to see.

Answers:
1 $4,000
2 $350
3 $20,000
4 £1,065
5 ¥15,000

Look and learn

Books open. Model the numbers slowly and clearly. Take care to differentiate between *fifteen* and *fifty* thousand. Some students may be confused by *fifteen hundred*: explain that one thousand five hundred is also acceptable (U.K. English) but that standard American English would be *fifteen hundred*.

Take care with this drill. The Japanese system of counting reads large numbers not in thousands but in ten thousands, and so numbers over 10,000 in English are very difficult for Japanese students. If your class is totally confused, tell the class to close their books, and spend time building up the chart on the board. Take care over the pronunciation of **thousand**. Explain how to say percentages: 10% = *ten percent*, 2.5% = *two point five percent*. Write some percentages on the board and ask students to say them.

When students are ready, go into the practice phase.

Books open. Read the instructions under the chart. Demonstrate with a student and, if necessary, teach *Yes, that's right! / No. Try again.* for the students to use with their partners. Give them plenty of time to practice.

Optional Activities

Bingo!

Write a list of about twenty large numbers on the board randomly. Include some numbers that are easy to confuse (e.g., 13,000, 1,300, 30,000). Tell students to copy down five of the numbers onto scrap paper. This is their "bingo card". Read out the numbers in random order, making a note of the ones you say. If you say a number that the student has written down, he/she crosses it off his/her list. The first student to cross out all five numbers calls out Bingo! and is the winner.

Play the game twice using the same or new numbers. Students make new bingo cards. (If your class deliberately writes down the easier numbers, ask students to swap cards with their partner – they usually then try to choose the most difficult numbers for their friend!)

Fake money

If you are teaching in Japan, it is quite easy to buy toy Japanese yen in toy shops or convenience stores. Hand out miscellaneous amounts of yen to each student and drill: *How much do you have? I have … yen.*

Students count their "money" and answer their partner's question. This can be repeated several times, with you handing out more money, or students swapping bills among themselves. This provides good practice of large numbers. Listen carefully to ensure that students are pronouncing **yen** in the English way.

Conversation

Hold your book so that the students can see p. 11. Say: *Look at page 11. Look at the "Conversation."* Read the instructions aloud and when everyone is ready, play the cassette.

Tell the students to check their answers together. Say: *Work together in pairs. Check your answers. Do you have the same answers?*

Say: *Now listen again.* Play the cassette again, this time pausing after the three blanks to give the students time to check their answers. If necessary, play the tape a third time.

After the students have checked their answers together, nominate students to tell you the answers and write them on the board. Tell the class that *percent* is the same in Japanese as in English, but that students should be careful with their pronunciation (they may say *percento*).

Answers:
1 ¥20,000
2 2 percent
3 $196

Books closed. Model or use the cassette to drill the conversation chorally. Watch out for problems with *commission, exchange , percent*, and *196 dollars*. Most students will be able to understand *exchange rate* from the context, but you may wish to take in a newspaper to show the students some examples and to tell them the current rate. Explain that *commission* is the money that the bank charges and that it often varies from place to place.

After sufficient drilling, tell the students to look again at p. 11 and to practice the conversation in pairs, using the "read, look up and speak" technique. If you have toy money, hand out amounts and have the students act out the conversation.

Over to you!

Say: *Now practice the "Conversation" again. Make four new conversations, using this information.* Students should be used to this type of activity by now and be able to proceed without any difficulties. Pre-teach *point* as in *1.5 %* (*one point five percent*). Monitor to check that students are able to produce the numbers confidently. Offer help and corrections as necessary. Students should practice several times, until they can do the conversation smoothly, maintaining eye contact as much as possible.

Give feedback at the end of the activity. If necessary, return to *Look and learn* briefly to reinforce numbers and to remind students of their pronunciation.

Nominate pairs of students to act out their conversations for the class: for large classes, have several groups perform at the same time so as not to intimidate the speakers.

Optional Activity

Pounds and pence

Students who are planning to visit the U.K. may prefer to practice the conversation substituting *pounds* in place of *dollars*. Model the correct pronunciation of *pounds* (not *ponds*), and write these prompts on the board for students to use instead of (or in addition to) the prompts given in the book:

1	¥10,000	¥20,000	¥75,000	¥40,000
2	2 %	1.5%	2.5%	3%
3	£65	£131	£487	£258

(Based on an exchange rate of ¥150 to the pound.)

Activity

New partners. Say: *Cover the words*. Gesture to show that students should cover the *Look and learn* and *Conversation* sections. Read the instructions aloud and allocate roles. Confident students should stand up and act out the conversation as best they can. Encourage higher-level groups to improvise as much as possible. Point to the emergency language posters on the walls to remind students not to revert to Japanese when they are struggling. If you are met with a distressed silence after setting up the activity, give the bank clerks a few phrases to start off the conversation: *Good afternoon. Can I help you?*

Monitor the activity and note any persistent errors. After practicing several times, using a range of amounts on the exchange rate chart, have the students change roles and partners for further practice. If you have toy money, hand it out for the customers to use.

When the activity winds down naturally, congratulate the students and have them return to their seats. On the board, write some of the mistakes you heard and have the students work in pairs to correct them. Say: *Here are some of the mistakes I heard. Can*

you correct them? Give them a few minutes to complete the task. Elicit the correct answers and correct the sentences on the board.

Finishing the lesson

Bring the class back together and have the students return to their seats. Tell them to look again at the *Background notes* for Unit 3. List the functions on the board and elicit an example for each one. Write the examples up too, e.g.:

> Understanding amounts of money:
> *That comes to 150 dollars.*
> Asking about exchange rates:
> *What's the exchange rate?*
> Asking about commission:
> *How much commission do you charge?*

Tell the students to copy down the examples. Assign any review homework you feel is necessary. Tell the class that in the next lesson they will learn how to reserve a room in a hotel.

Ask the class to read the *Background notes* for Unit 4 before the next class.

Optional Activity

Review: large numbers

(Only for classes on good terms with each other!) Pre-teach this mini conversation:

> A: I really like your jacket!
> B: Oh, do you?
> A: Yes, it's really cool. Do you mind me asking, how much did it cost?
> B: Of course not. I think it was about ¥12,000.
> A: Really? Thanks!
> B: You're welcome.

Students work with a friend and practice the dialog, referring to real objects they can see (suit, tie, earrings, etc.) or imaginary ones (house, car, golf clubs, etc.). Be careful to remind students to change the conversation if they refer to plural items. This is a fun, non-threatening way to practice large numbers.

Unit 4
Do you have any vacancies?

| **Topic / functions** |
| Asking about vacancies |
| Checking prices |
| Asking for a room |

Review

Changing money at the bank: scrambled sentences
Write these scrambled sentences on the board and ask students to work in pairs to put them in the right order.

1 today exchange the rate What is ?
2 do you How charge much commission ?
3 some here money Can change I ?
4 $200 comes That to

Changing money at the bank: dialog
Books closed. Write on the board:

¥45,000 = $441 ¥100 = $1.00 Commission: 2%

Tell the students to work in pairs to make a short conversation in the bank, using the information given. If the group struggles, allow them to glance again at *Look and learn* in Unit 3. However, having just unscrambled the key sentences, most groups should be able to cope satisfactorily.

Warming up

Preview: Background notes for Unit 4
Books closed. Tell the students that in this unit, they will meet Mayumi and Makoto. Ask if anyone can remember which country they are visiting (the U.K.).

Remind the class that Mayumi and Makoto are on their honeymoon and are visiting many countries in Europe. Ask where they think Mayumi and Makoto will stay, to elicit *a hotel*. Write *Places to stay* on the board and ask students to brainstorm in pairs different places you can stay when traveling abroad. The *Background notes* list a variety of places, and students should be able to remember some, e.g., *hotel, hostel, motel, bed and breakfast*. Write answers on the board.

If you can, bring in newspapers, tourist hotel pamphlets, etc., to show your students how to find out about places to stay. Tourist information offices and travel agencies are good sources of this type of material. Remind students that with more expensive package tours, accommodation is usually pre-arranged, but if they decide to spend a few days traveling around, they will need to reserve a room.

Pre-teach: *a single room*, *a double room*, *number of nights*, *vacancy*. Write these words on the board and ask students to write it down in their vocabulary books.

Open your books

Tell the students to look at the picture on p. 12 of their books. Read the unit title. Ask the students who Mayumi is talking to, to elicit *a hotel clerk*. Read the caption aloud: *Mayumi and Makoto are planning a trip to Oxford. Mayumi is reserving a hotel room.*

Listening

Read through the instructions with the students, checking that everyone remembers the meaning of *true* and *false* from Unit 2 by making a few statements about yourself (*My name is... / I'm from...*, etc.) and eliciting a response from different students. When everyone is ready, play the cassette and monitor to check that everyone understands and is completing the task. Tell the students: *Work in pairs. Check your answers. Do you have the same answers?*

Say: *Now listen again.* Play the cassette again, this time pausing after each dialog. If the group is having difficulties, replay the key sentences (*A double room?* etc.) and pause after playing them.

Tell the students to check again in pairs. Play the tape one more time, and elicit the answers by taking a class vote. If the entire class chooses the wrong answer, replay the relevant part, pause the tape, and repeat the sentences slowly. Write the answers on the board.

Answers:
1 T **2** F **3** F **4** F **5** T **6** T

Look and learn

Books closed. Model the questions and answers clearly but at normal speed and with natural intonation. Use a substitution drill to drill the questions and answers chorally, gesturing for students to repeat after you.

Substitution drill:

T: *Do you have any vacancies for tonight?*
SS: *Do you have any vacancies for tonight?*
T: *rooms*
SS: *Do you have any rooms for tonight?*
T: *Friday*
SS: *Do you have any rooms for Friday?*
T: *vacancies*

SS: *Do you have any vacancies for Friday?*
T: *tomorrow*
SS: *Do you have any vacancies for tomorrow?*

Continue in the same way. Substitution drills can be quite confusing for students unless they are set up very carefully. In particular, the teacher's body language needs to be very clear. Teach your class what your signals are for "repeat", "reply", "change the sentence", "ask him/her", etc. This is worth spending some time on, as drills are a very time-efficient way to practice new language and to allow the students to practice the new sounds, stress and intonation patterns. Bear in mind, however, that drills only work if the students understand what they are practicing: the example above requires some thought on the part of the students to ensure that they substitute the correct part of the sentence.

Do not overdo the drills, however (there is a long-standing EFL joke that "drills are a device for boring!"). After practicing all the questions and answers in *Look and learn*, have students open their books to p. 12 and practice the questions and answers in pairs.

Optional Activities

Days and dates

Higher-level classes may start substituting different information into the questions and answers. Check that your whole class knows the months of the year. Ask the class to stand in a line in order of their birthdays. Students need to ask When's your birthday? to do this; insist that they use English! Do a quick check down the line when students are rearranged. If there is any confusion, write the months on the board, as well as numbers 1st–31st. Drill if necessary.

Tell students to practice the language study again, but to change some of the information and use their own names.

Prices practice

Having practiced large numbers in the previous unit, you may wish to spend a short time checking that your students are confident in talking about prices. Write the following prices on the board:

$90	£25.00	¥10,000
$150	£50.75	¥7,500
$75.99	£12.50	¥6,800
$45.00	£15.00	¥12,300

If your students are all going to one destination, use the currency of that country. Have the students practice saying the prices in pairs: *How much is the room? It's … per night.* After letting them practice for a few minutes, nominate pairs around the class to ask and answer, as you point to each price in turn.

Conversation

Hold your book so that the students can see p. 13. Say: *Look at page 13. Look at the "Conversation."* Read the instructions aloud and point to the picture again on p. 12 of the Student Book to remind the students about Mayumi. If your class has been coping well with the *Conversation* listenings so far, go straight into playing the tape without reading through the dialog first. Say: *Listen to the cassette. Write your answers. … Now check together in pairs. Do you have the same answers?*

Say: *Now listen again.* Replay the conversation, pausing after the blanks so that students have time to change their answers if they wish. If necessary, play the tape one more time without stopping.

Elicit the answers by asking different students to read the conversation line by line around the class. Write the answers on the board so that students can check their spelling.

Answers:
1 Thursday
2 double
3 two nights
4 £76
5 Kinoshita
6 K–I–N–O–S–H–I–T–A
7 0181 342 9799

Books closed. Model the conversation, or use the cassette, to drill in chorus. Students may have problems with the pronunciation of *vacancies*, the elision in *could you*, and spelling their names out.

Optional Activity

The alphabet

It is worth spending a few minutes to point out common errors which Japanese students make in pronouncing certain letters, and warning your students to be careful with those sounds. The most common mistakes are:

● *b* and *v* confusion. Model the sounds clearly and have the students take note of the position of your lips for these letters. Many students say the letter *v* as something close to *voo-ee*. Teach your class to say *vee*. Using small mirrors may help.

● The letter *c* is often pronounced *she* rather than *see*. Teach students where to position their tongue when saying *see*.

● The letter *r* is often pronounced as *er* rather than *ar*. Model the correct mouth shape.

● The letter *w* is often said simply as *double*, instead of being read as *double-u* . This can cause great confusion when spelling things over the phone!

● Remind students that the letter *z* can be pronounced *zee* (U.S.) or *zed* (U.K.).

Having practiced these letters, teach your class how to spell their names out clearly, grouping several letters together, using intonation appropriate for listing things, rather than spelling out one letter at a time in an unending stream. Consider which is easier to write down:

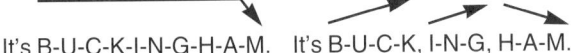

It's B-U-C-K-I-N-G-H-A-M.   It's B-U-C-K, I-N-G, H-A-M.

Teach your students how to use the word *double* correctly, e.g., *ll = double l.*

Have your students practice spelling their names, friends' names, and family's names to their partner, who writes them down. If your classroom allows, have students sit back-to-back to simulate a telephone conversation. Encourage students to use emergency language to ask for repetitions where necessary.

You may wish to practice giving telephone numbers in the same way. Again, teach the correct use of *double* as in *99 = double nine.* (Be careful not to confuse your class when teaching all these different "doubles". You do not want students to start saying *double-u nine* for 99!)

Books open. Have the students sit back-to-back to practice the *Conversation*. Even though the students clearly can't make eye contact in this situation, still encourage the learners to "read, look up, and speak" to reduce dependence upon the written word. Monitor and offer help and corrections where necessary.

Over to you!

The class should be comfortable with this type of exercise by now. Put the class in pairs and have them practice. Listen to check that the prices are not causing difficulties and that everyone can say *Wednesday*. Have some pairs act out the dialogs for the rest of the class.

Activity

New partners. Say: *Cover the words.* Gesture to show that students should cover the *Look and learn* and *Conversation* sections. Read the instructions aloud and allocate roles. If possible, have the students sit back-to-back to practice telephoning. Monitor and note any problems with dates, spelling, question formation and telephone numbers. Remind students that in the U.K. and Australia they should ask for a *twin room* if they want two beds. A *double room* would usually have just one large bed in it. (This is explained in the *Background notes.*)

Give feedback at the end of the *Activity* and ask some students to perform their telephone conversations for the class.

Finishing the lesson

Bring the class back together after the *Activity* and congratulate them for their efforts. Tell the students to look again at the *Background notes* for Unit 4. List the functions on the board and elicit an example for each one. Write the examples too, e.g.:

Asking about vacancies:
Do you have any vacancies for tonight?
Checking prices:
How much is the room?
Asking for a room:
I'd like a single room, please.

Tell the students to copy down the examples. Assign any review homework you feel is necessary. Tell the class that in the next lesson, they will learn how to ask for and understand directions.

Ask the class to read the *Background notes* for Unit 5 before the next class.

Optional Activity

Review: Scrambled sentences

Write these scrambled sentences on the board and ask students to work in pairs to decode them.

1 have Do rooms tomorrow you any for ?
2 nights many how For ?
3 like single a please I'd
4 time arrive What you will ?
5 6 P.M. At around
6 check just I'll

Answers:

1 Do you have any rooms for tomorrow?
2 For how many nights?
3 I'd like a single, please.
4 What time will you arrive?
5 At around 6 P.M.
6 I'll just check.

Unit 5
Go straight along Seventh Avenue

Topic / functions
Asking for directions
Giving directions
Saying where places are

Review

Drawing game: vocabulary from Unit 4
Write these words on pieces of cardboard or paper:

vacancy	motel
price	night
single room	clerk
telephone number	arrive
homestay	bed

Divide your class into teams and give each team member a number. Have all the number 1 students come up to the board and show them one of the words. The students have to draw the word, without using letters or numbers. Their teammates watch and call out what they think the drawing is. The first team to answer correctly scores 5 points. Repeat the process with the number 2 students and a new word. Continue until you have used all the cards. This warm-up taps into your students' artistic abilities and gives an indication of whether your students have understood previously taught lexis.

Words chosen do not have to be concrete nouns. Set up the activity by starting a drawing and having the students guess what it is. *Travel* is a good example (draw Japan, another country, an arrow connecting the two, a plane, etc.). This activity generates a great deal of other vocabulary as students try to guess the word (e.g., *tourist, vacation, overseas, ticket, flight*).

Optional Activity

Drawing game: vocabulary from Units 1–4
If the drawing game works well with your group, and your scheduling allows, you may wish to spend a few minutes on a vocabulary review of the whole first four units. Set it up as above. Possible words to review:

newspaper	immigration officer	passport
flight attendant	occupation	money
pillow	student	bank
understand	homestay	traveler's check
Here you are	family	exchange rate
identification	price	night
coin	single room	clerk
percent	telephone number	arrive
sign	blanket	bed
vacancy	motel	

Choose the most useful words for your group from the list and play the game.

Warming up

Preview: Background notes for Unit 5
Books closed. Draw a stick picture of someone looking at a map, looking confused. Ask students who they would ask if they got lost (e.g., police officer, tourist information employee, store clerk). Tell the students that in this unit, Rie is trying to go sightseeing in New York.

Open your books

Point to the picture of Rie looking at the map on p. 14. Read the caption aloud: *Rie is asking for directions*.

Listening

Read through the instructions. Make sure that all the students understand that they have to circle the place on the map and that the starting point is the Hotel Gorham. Have students point at the hotel to check that everyone knows where to begin from. When everyone is ready, play the cassette through once without stopping. Students will probably have difficulties the first time, but by the third or fourth replay they should be able to cope. Say: *Work in pairs. Check your answers together. Did you circle the same places?*

Say: *Now listen again.* Play the cassette again, this time pausing after each dialog. After listening, let the students check together again. If they are still having difficulties, replay the tape, pausing after each new piece of information, and indicate the route on the map.

Play the cassette one last time and elicit the answers.

Answers:
1 Carnegie Hall
2 Coliseum Books
3 Russian Tea Room
4 McDonalds

Look and learn

Books closed. Drill the three questions. Then ask students to open their books to p. 14. Say: *Look at the diagrams.* Read the directions aloud and have the students repeat them. Beware of pronunciation problems caused by reading the words on the page: *straight, right*, and *th* in *57th* and *58th Street*.

If you prefer to drill the directions without the students reading from the page, draw similar pictures on the board and use these to drill the target language.

After sufficient practice, have the students take turns in pairs covering the words and pointing to a picture to test their partner. Remind them to use *Yes, that's right.* or *No, try again.*

Optional Activities

Map drawing

Draw a large, grid-style street map on the board and label the streets. Put in a number of squares to represent different buildings. Ask the students to tell you what these buildings are. False-beginner level students will come up with a surprisingly large amount of vocabulary in this brainstorming activity, e.g., *a bank, a post office, a pub, a temple, a pachinko parlor, a school, a sports club, a convenience store, a department store, a station, a fast-food restaurant, a hotel.*

As the students call out their ideas, write the names on the different buildings. Use the map to practice the target structures in *Look and learn*. Do a few examples first yourself:

A: *Excuse me. Do you know where the hotel is?*
B: *Yes. It's across from the pachinko parlor.*

A: *Can you help me? How do I get to ...?*
B: *Yes, it's ...*

Tell the students which building to use as a starting point. Have the students practice in pairs.

The furniture game

For small classes only. Have half the class leave the room briefly while the students who stay behind rearrange the furniture to make a simple obstacle course. Bring the other students into the room with their eyes closed (or use blindfolds) and pair them up with a student in the room. The students with their eyes open must give directions in English to their partner, to direct them across the room, without touching any of the desks or chairs. (Teach *Stop!* to cover any emergencies!) This game only practices *Turn left, Turn right*, and *Go straight*, but is a lot of fun for small classes who trust each other.

The area around here

For more able groups only. If your school is in a busy area and the students are familiar with it, students can interview each other about buildings nearby, e.g.:

A: *Can you help me? Do you know where the station is?*
B: *Yes, it's across from Odakyu Department Store. Go straight along Sakura Street for about five minutes. It's on the left.*

Conversation

Hold your book so that the students can see p. 15. Say: *Look at page 15. Look at the "Conversation."* Read the instructions aloud and check that everyone is ready to start. Play the tape through once without stopping. Let the students check in pairs, and play the tape again, this time pausing after each blank. Then read aloud the instructions under the dialog: *Check the directions on the map of New York.*

Have the students check their answers in pairs. Replay the cassette if any students are having difficulties.

Play the cassette one last time, stopping after each set of directions. Indicate the route on the map or ask a student to do so. Finally, write the answers on the board.

Answers:
1 Do you
2 right
3 Sixth Avenue
4 third right
5 left

Books closed. Model the conversation, or use the cassette, to drill in chorus. After sufficient practice, have students practice the conversation in pairs. Ensure that they change roles, as Rie's responses are short.

Optional Activity

Directions / Locations snap!

Put students in small groups and make one copy of photocopiable pages C and D (pp. 82-83) for each group. Cut them up to make into playing cards. Students shuffle the cards and deal all the cards out, face down, to the group. In turn, each student turns up a card and places it face up in the center. If they have a picture, they do not say anything. If they have a sentence, they should read it aloud. If a card is followed by its matching picture or words, the first students to shout *Snap!* collects all the cards which have been laid down. If someone makes a mistake, they must forfeit two cards into the center pile.

Over to you!

Ask the students to look again at the map on p. 14 of their books. Write on the board the following places: The Hard Rock Café, New York Visitors' Bureau, The Gap, The Hotel Ritz Carlton. Say: *Work in pairs. Start at the Hotel Gorham. Ask your partner how to get to these places.*

Monitor the exercise and make notes on any serious errors. Offer help as necessary and, at the end of the activity, give feedback on any mistakes. Directions are often difficult for native speakers to give clearly, so congratulate students who manage to give comprehensible answers.

Activity

Remind the students that Koji is in Sydney, Australia, on a Working Holiday Visa. Say: *Look at page 15. Look at the map of Sydney.* If any of your students have been to Sydney, ask them which places they remember from the map. Tell the class that Centrepoint is the tallest tower in the Southern Hemisphere and is a famous tourist attraction.

Students should look at the map and use Centrepoint as the starting point for the activity.

New pairs. Read the instructions aloud and have the class make new conversations. If this seems too free for your class, list some of the places marked on the map on the board as prompts. Encourage eye contact and remind students to use emergency language if they have problems (*I'm sorry, could you repeat that, please?* etc.).

When the activity winds down, congratulate the students. On the board, write some of the mistakes you heard and have the students work in pairs to correct them. Say: *Here are some of the mistakes I heard. Can you correct them?* Give the students a few minutes to complete the task. Some of the most common mistakes will involve using the wrong article, omitting the article, and using incorrect word order (e.g., *Do you know where is the hotel?*). Elicit the correct answers and correct the sentences on the board.

Optional Activity

Pairwork map activity

The map activities in this unit provide very simple practice, as both students can look at the map and see where the place is. Classes who coped well with these exercises may benefit from the information-gap map activity on photocopiable page E (p. 84). Make one copy of the page for each pair of students in the class and cut them in half.

Put students in pairs and read the instructions. Make sure that they cannot see their partner's page. Check that all students know what to do and, if necessary,

demonstrate with a student. Books should be closed at this point, but some weaker learners may be happier if they can use the *Look and learn* diagrams for occasional reference. Monitor and offer help and corrections as necessary. Let students compare their maps at the end of the exercise.

Finishing the Lesson

Bring the class back together. Congratulate the class. Tell the students to look again at the *Background notes* for Unit 5. List the functions on the board and elicit an example for each one. Write the examples too, e.g.:

Asking for directions:
   How do I get to the post office?
Giving directions:
   Go straight ahead.
Saying where places are:
   It's next to the bank.

Tell the students to copy down the examples. Assign any review homework you feel is necessary. If you are planning to go straight onto Unit 6 next time, tell the class that they will learn how to ask a homestay family about house rules, and ask the class to read the *Background notes* for Unit 6 before the next lesson. If you are going to spend a whole lesson on the first *Out and About* page, leave the *Background notes* reading homework for next time.

Optional Activity

Review: picture captions

Draw the diagrams from *Look and learn* on the board. Tell the students to work in pairs to try to work out the directions and locations they represent. Ask different students to come to the board and write the captions under each picture. Correct at the end as necessary.

Out and About 1
Sightseeing

Read through the notes in the introduction on p. 7 first, for additional ideas on how to use the *Out and About* pages. This unit is particularly appropriate for work using tourist brochures, promotional videos, etc., as all five characters are seen in famous tourist spots in the countries they are visiting.

If your students will all be visiting the same place abroad, use this lesson as an opportunity to tell them a little about some of the places worth visiting. For groups who do not yet have plans to go abroad, if you have the realia on hand, bring in maps and brochures of a variety of places, and have the students work in small groups to plan short trips and itineraries. Use the *Out and About* pages to give your class a sense of the places they can visit using the survival English they are learning in *Passport*. Any students who have already been abroad can be interviewed by their classmates in small groups about the places where they went sightseeing and the language that was most useful.

Tell the students to look at the pictures on pp. 16–17. Use a world map to show them the countries/cities the characters are visiting. Ask them to tell you where they are, and to name the places shown. They are:

- Sydney Opera House, Sydney, Australia
- the Statue of Liberty, New York, U.S.
- Harrods, London, U.K.
- Ayers Rock, Northern Territory, Australia
- the Golden Gate Bridge, San Francisco, U.S.
- Buckingham Palace, London, U.K.

Have the students read the conversations. Explain any difficult vocabulary, e.g.:

brochure	pamphlet (bring in an example)
bargains	something at a very good price
taxi stand	the place where you catch a taxi (c.f., bus stop, train station)
cheese	tell the students to watch your mouth as you say cheese – you smile!
Slip, Slop, Slap	demonstrate the actions and explain that this is a slogan from an Australian campaign to reduce skin cancer incidents
sunburn(t)	many students mistake *suntan* for *sunburn*. Explain the difference clearly. Teach *sunbathing* (also often mistakenly referred to by students as *sunburning*!).

Model the mini-dialogs. Point out that Koji and Miki use *Thank you* to be polite and that when Miki asks someone to take a picture, she says *Excuse me* first. Remind the class that when they talk to strangers, the more polite the better. Drill as necessary.

Have the students practice the short conversations. Encourage them to memorize the ones they consider most useful. Ask some pairs to act out their dialogs. Higher-level classes can lengthen the dialogs by adding more information and/or continuing the conversations.

Write five or six more typical sightseeing situations on the board, e.g., looking for a restroom, asking when the store closes, asking how much the postcards cost, checking the time of the last bus, buying a student ticket for a show, paying by traveler's check, etc.

Put the students into small groups and tell them to write and practice mini-dialogs for two of the situations. Monitor and offer help as necessary. Have some groups perform their role-plays for the rest of the group at the end of the activity. Give feedback at the end.

Unit 6
Do you mind if I watch TV?

Topic / functions
Checking house rules

Asking for help

Finding out the best time to do something

Review

Giving directions
Ask the class to look back at the map of New York on p. 14. Tell them that the starting point is the Hotel Ritz Carlton. Students work in pairs and ask for directions to three places each. More able groups should attempt this with the *Look and learn* diagrams covered, but let weaker groups use the diagrams for reference. Don't spend too long on this activity, however. Directions take a long time for false beginners to feel comfortable with, and you don't want to put them off at the first step!

Warming up

Preview: Background notes for Unit 6
Books closed. Remind the class about the *Background notes* they read for Unit 6. Ask some general questions to jog students' memories, especially if you assigned this reading homework prior to studying the *Out and About* unit. Questions might include:

Where is Koji? Is he staying in a hotel?

What's the name of his homestay family?

Have you ever been on a homestay program?

What are the differences between staying in a hotel and staying with a family?

What kinds of jobs around the house should you help with when you stay with a family?

When you arrive at your homestay family's house, what things will you want to ask them about, around the house?

Do not expect complete answers at this stage. Accept any relevant one-word answers like *bathroom, mealtimes, telephone,* etc.

With higher-level groups, you may want to spend some time talking about cultural differences between Japanese homes and Western homes. Table manners, food, and gift-giving at the end of the stay are covered

in other units, so try to steer the topic towards general behavior around the home, what happens in different rooms in the house, and so on. Teacher-talk about your own home is very interesting for students, especially if you have some photographs to show them.

If your artistic skills are reasonably good, draw a large cross section of a Western-style house on the board, with simple furniture in some of the rooms (e.g., a bathtub and shower, a dining table and chairs, a sofa and television, a washing machine, a microwave oven, a kettle, a telephone, a bed). Teach the names of different rooms around the house if students do not know them and use the picture to elicit or brainstorm furniture vocabulary.

Pre-teach *washing machine, microwave, TV, shower, bath,* and *telephone* before starting the listening task. Magazine advertisements are a good source for pictures of furniture, but stick drawings usually work just as well. For higher-level groups, you do not need to use the pictures. Instead, scramble the words and put them on the board. Tell the students that these are items that you can find in the home. Students should guess what they are. Do the first one as an example, e.g.:

hsiwang chimaen   *washing machine.*

Open your books

Tell the students to look at the picture of Koji on p. 18 of their books. Read the unit title and the caption: *Koji is talking to his host family.* Tell the students to work in pairs and see how many things in the picture they can name.

Listening
Read the instructions aloud. Tell the students to listen very carefully to Koji. He talks about many things, but what is he asking questions about?

Play the tape and stop after the first dialog. Have the students check their answer together and replay if there is confusion. The first time through, some students may struggle, as both words (*microwave* and *washing machine*) are heard in the dialog. The key is that students have to listen out for the question Koji asks. If your group is weak, do the first one as an example, focusing upon *Can you show me how to use the washing machine?*

Play the dialogs through once, without stopping. Tell the students: *Work in pairs. Check your answers together. Do you have the same answers?*

Say: *Now listen again.* Replay the tape, this time pausing after each dialog. If the group is having difficulties, replay the key sentences and pause after playing them. Tell the students to check again in pairs.

Play the tape one more time, and elicit the answers by nominating students. Write the answers on the board.

Answers:
1   the washing machine
2   a blanket
3   the TV
4   a shower
5   smoking
6   the telephone

Optional Activity

Using the tapescript

More able groups may benefit from looking over the tapescript for this unit. This is the first unit that starts to "stretch" the students, and there are many features of natural speech in the homestay dialogs that can be pointed out to the class. Lower-level classes will only be confused by the tapescript, however, which has a lot of extra information that they do not need to understand to complete the task, and it is better not to use the tapescript in these cases.

Look and learn

Books closed. If possible, use large magazine pictures of a television, shower, cigarette, telephone, and bathtub while drilling the sentences. These pictures can then be used as prompts later. Drill:

T: *Do you mind if I watch TV?*
SS: *Do you mind if I watch TV?*
T: *take a shower?*
SS: *Do you mind if I take a shower?*

Continue like this, and practice the answers:

T: *Not at all.*
SS: *Not at all.*
T: (holding up picture of TV) *Yasuko, ask Keiko.*
Yasuko: *Do you mind if I watch TV?*
Keiko: *Not at all.*

Not at all is notoriously problematic for students. Teach the class that a common reply to *Do you mind…?* is *Not at all* and that it means, *Yes, go ahead.* Draw smiling and frowning faces on the board to show if a response is positive or negative. *I'd rather you didn't* is a negative response and is more polite than a direct *No.*

Drill all the questions and answers. Explain *collect call* (U.S. English; U.K. English is *reverse charge call*) and any other problem areas. Listen to check that students do not start using *Not at all* with the wrong question (e.g., * *Could I take a shower now? Not at all.*)

After modeling and practicing the *Look and learn* section, have students open their books to p. 18 and practice in pairs. Encourage repetition so that the

students start to internalize the target language. Have them practice with different partners if necessary.

Conversation

Hold your book so that the students can see p. 19. Say: *Look at page 19. Look at the "Conversation."* Read the instructions aloud and point to the picture on p. 18 of the Student Book to show the students who Mrs. Todd is (the host mother). Your class should have no problems understanding the task by this stage in the book. Play the cassette and monitor to check that everyone is filling in the blanks.

Have the students check together. Replay the cassette and pause after each blank. If necessary, play the tape through one more time without stopping. Elicit the answers and write them on the board. Some students will have problems spelling *towel.*

Answers:
1   take a bath
2   a towel
3   the shower
4   go out this evening
5   don't be late home

Explain *front door key* and *back door key*. Point out that *go out* is a very common expression (*going out with my friends, going out for dinner, going out for a drink, Are you going out tonight?* etc.). If your students translate directly from Japanese, they usually say *I played with my friends* or similar. Explain that *play* in English is usually used only for children, or for some sports, and that *go out* is more appropriate.

Books closed. Model the conversation, or use the cassette to drill it chorally. Model the correct pronunciation of *Do you, Could you,* and *Don't be.* Model the correct intonation patterns so that students sound polite as they ask the questions. This is usually a matter of pitch (a high pitch at the start of the question sounds polite) and appropriate hesitation: students should not sound abrupt when they ask *Could you show me…?*

Books open. Have the students practice the conversation in pairs, using the "read, look up and speak" technique.

Over to you!

Put students in pairs and have them practice the conversation, substituting the new information. Pre-teach and model *laundry, detergent,* and *kettle.* Monitor for good intonation patterns. If students start getting monotonal, re-drill using exaggerated intonation/pitch to encourage students to use their voices well. Have some pairs act out their conversations for the rest of the class.

Optional Activity

Social chit-chat

If you have time in your schedule to use supplementary activities, use photocopiable page F (p. 85) to help students with some of the day-to-day formulaic language that they may need to use with their homestay families. Make one copy for each pair of students. Have the students work in pairs to guess at the replies, but not write them in.

After a few minutes, elicit possible replies and offer some of your own. Write these on the board and have the students fill in the blank speech bubbles. This is a good exercise to do prior to the *Activity* in the Student Book. Higher-level classes will be able to use some of the new expressions in their role-plays.

Activity

New partners. Tell the students to cover the *Conversation* and *Look and Learn* and to look at the pictures. Allocate roles and read the instructions aloud. Give the students a few minutes to think about what they want to say and remind them to be polite as they ask and answer. Some students may revert to saying *I want… / No, you can't* when put on the spot. Note these types of error and give feedback at the end of the activity. Explain that while *I want to watch TV* is grammatically correct, *Do you mind…?* is polite and more appropriate to use with a homestay family.

Optional Activity

Did you sleep well?

Higher-level classes, especially if you have used photocopiable page F with the group, should be encouraged to role-play their conversations, using English as much as possible. You may wish to have students listen to the first conversations in the *Listening* section of the unit one more time as an example.

Arrange the chairs to represent a living room or kitchen and tell students the situation, e.g., You are having breakfast; You have just come home after going shopping; It's 9 P.M. and the family is watching TV. Put students in pairs or small groups and allocate roles (host mother, father, or student). You may wish to take a role yourself briefly with some groups to get them started. This type of role-play can be very difficult for false-beginner level students, particularly as there is no obvious end to the task, i.e., they don't know when they have finished. In previous units, when they have completed the transaction, such as changing money in the bank, the students know that the activity is over.

If your class is very uncomfortable with this amount of freedom, writing word prompts on the board can make the role-play more concrete. However, more able groups should try to get used to this freer stage. In real

life, conversations are unstructured and often open-ended, and the activity aims to give students as realistic a practice phase as is possible under classroom conditions.

Monitor and make mental notes of any important errors. Give feedback at the end of the activity. Confident groups can show their role-plays to the rest of the class.

Finishing the lesson

Bring the class back together and congratulate them on their efforts. Tell the class to look again at the *Background notes* for Unit 6. List the functions on the board and elicit an example for each one. Write the examples too, e.g.:

Checking house rules:
Do you mind if I smoke in my room?
Asking for help:
Could you show me how to use the washing machine?
Finding out the best time to do something:
Can I take a shower tomorrow morning?

Tell the students to copy down the examples. Assign any review homework you feel is necessary. Tell the class that in the next lesson, they will learn what to do if they feel ill while traveling abroad.

Ask the class to read the *Background notes* for Unit 7 before the next class.

Optional Activity

Review: match the sentences

Write these questions and answers on the board and ask the class to copy them down. Tell students to match them by drawing lines, and then to practice asking and answering in pairs.

The questions:

1 Do you mind if I take a shower before dinner?
2 Is it OK if I call my mother in Japan today?
3 Could you show me how to use the washing machine, please?
4 Is it OK if I watch TV now?
5 Could you show me how to use the microwave, please?

The answers:

a Sure. What are you going to watch?
b Sure. Do you have a lot of laundry?
c Yes, of course. I think the cheap rate is after 11 P.M..
d Go ahead.
e No problem. What are you cooking?

Answers: 1 d 2 c 3 b 4 a 5 e

Unit 7
How do you feel?

Topic / functions
Saying what's wrong

Saying when the problem began

Understanding instructions

Review

Staying with a family
Put these words up on the board:

laundry	detergent
washing machine	thank you
show	call Japan
Not at all	cheap rate

Books closed. Tell the students to work in pairs and to make a short conversation using all the words on the board. If the group struggles, allow them to look briefly at *Look and learn* to remind themselves of possible question and answer structures.

Warming up

Preview: Background notes for Unit 7
Books closed. Remind the students about the background reading they did for Unit 7. Ask the class why people sometimes get sick when they travel overseas (e.g., different food, change in climate, not enough sleep, too much alcohol!). Tell the class that in this unit, Mayumi goes to the doctor because she has a stomachache. Mime *stomachache* for the class.

If your class is weak, point to yourself or draw a large outline of a person on the board and label it, to teach the following parts of the body: *head*, *back*, *stomach*, *ear*, *tooth*, *throat*, *shoulder*, *leg*, *arm*. (Model the words before you write them down: *throat* is very difficult to pronounce while looking at the spelling!)

Optional Activity

Body parts
For classes who already know the parts of the body, play a brainstorming game in small groups. Ask groups of three or four to sit in a circle and to set up a clapping rhythm (e.g., slap thighs, clap hands, click fingers). Students take turns calling out a part of the body around the circle; the rhythm keeps the activity moving quickly. For example:

Slap, clap, click, (S1) *ARM!*

Slap, clap, click, (S2) *NOSE!*

Slap, clap, click, (S3) *THUMB!*,

Slap, clap, click, (S1) *STOMACH!*

At the end of the activity, list any extra useful vocabulary on the board and ask the class to copy it into their vocabulary books.

Explain the difference between *going to the doctor* and *going to the hospital*. (You go to the doctor if you have a stomachache, cold, or small illness; you go to the hospital if you break your leg, have an accident, or are very seriously ill.) Many students misuse the word *hospital* when they actually mean *doctor's office*.

Open your books

Ask the students to look at the picture of Mayumi on p. 20. Read the caption aloud: *Mayumi is at the doctor's.*

Listening
Read the instructions aloud and go through each of the sentences, pointing at the different parts of the body. Ask the students to check the correct boxes as they listen to the cassette. Play the cassette through once. Say: *Work in pairs. Check your answers together. Do you have the same answers?*

Say: *Now listen again.* Play the cassette again, this time stopping after each dialog to give the students time to check their answers. Encourage higher-level classes to listen for the questions the doctor asks while completing the task.

Tell the students to check together again in pairs. Elicit the correct answers by taking a class vote and write the answers on the board.

Answers:

1 a sore throat

2 an earache

3 a backache

4 a stomachache

Look and learn

Books closed. Drill the questions chorally. Nominate students to ask you the questions. Mime the problem or point to the affected part of the body and drill the problems in a four-step drill:

S: *What can I do for you?*
T: (mimes) *I have a headache.*
SS: *I have a headache.*
T: *I have a headache.*
S: *What seems to be the trouble?*
T: (mimes) *I have a sore throat.*
SS: *I have a sore throat.*
T: *I have a sore throat.*

After practicing all of the language in *Look and learn*, have the students look again at p. 20 and read through the list. Read the instructions under the language box and have the students practice in pairs.

Conversation

Hold your book so that the students can see p. 21. Say: *Look at page 21. Look at the "Conversation."* Read the instructions aloud and give the students time to complete the conversation by filling in the blanks speculatively. Stronger classes should be able to do this by themselves, but let less confident groups work in pairs. Pre-teach *painful, hurting, prescription,* and *before meals.*

Say: *Now listen. Check your answers. Did you get it right?* Play the cassette through once and have the students check together.

Say: *Now listen again.* Replay the cassette, pausing after each blank so that students have time to change their answers if they wish. If necessary, play the cassette one more time through without stopping.

Check the answers as a class. Write the whole conversation on the board and have different students fill in the blanks. Alternatively, nominate students to tell you the answers and write them on the board.

Answers:
1 b **2** d **3** a **4** c **5** e

Books closed. Model the conversation, or use the cassette, drilling in chorus. After sufficient practice, tell the students to practice in pairs, using the "read, look up and speak" technique.

Optional Activity

Guess the problem!: class game

Make enough copies of photocopiable page G (p.86) so that each student has one card. Students also need a piece of paper and a pen. Give them a few minutes to interview as many people as possible, asking *How do you feel? / What seems to be the trouble?*

In response to the question, students read out the information on their role cards but do not tell their partner what the specific problem is. The interviewer replies *Oh, I see. Take care of yourself!* and writes down the name of the person they spoke to and what they think the problem is.

After a few minutes, tell the class to return to their seats. Ask each student *What seems to be the trouble?* This time the students should read out the specific problem, printed at the bottom of the card. The rest of the class listens and checks their list. The winner is the person who guessed the most illnesses correctly. Students do not have to worry about spelling in this activity. The game is a fun way to have students listen to each other and make inferences from what they hear.

Over to you!

Books open to p. 21. Say: *Now practice the conversation again. Make three more conversations, using this information.*

Pre-teach *awful, twice a day, terrible, after meals, sore* and *once a day.*

Have the students practice with a new partner. Monitor and listen for pronunciation problems.

Nominate students to act out their conversations for the class.

Optional Activity

Giving advice

Higher-level groups only. Remind students that if they have a cold or headache, and it is not bad, they may not need to go to the doctor. Instead, their homestay family or a friend may be able to give them advice.

Model and drill the patterns: *Why don't you...?* and *I think you should...* and elicit examples of advice that friends might give, e.g., *go to bed, buy some throat drops, put ice on it, drink some warm milk, take some medicine.*

Put students in groups of three or four. Each student tells the group an imaginary problem and the other students give advice. Repeat several times and give feedback on mistakes at the end.

Activity

New partners. Tell students to cover the rest of the page and to look at the *Activity*. Read the instructions aloud and allocate roles. Confident students should stand up and act out the conversation, and very confident groups should be urged to use as much English as they can manage. If your group is more able, you may wish to replay the first listening activity before the students try out the exercise, to listen to any additional information that they might be able to use in the role-play (e.g., reasons why they feel ill). Give weaker groups a few sentences to get them started, e.g., *Good afternoon. Can I have your name, please?*

If you wish, ask confident pairs to perform their role-play to the rest of the class.

When the activity winds down naturally, congratulate the students and have them return to their seats. Give feedback on any important errors by writing them on the board and having the students correct them in pairs. Elicit the answers and correct the sentences on the board. Let students copy the sentences down.

Finishing the lesson

Tell the students to look again at the *Background notes* for Unit 7. List the functions on the board and elicit an example for each one. Write the examples too, e.g.:

Saying what's wrong:
I have a headache.
Saying when the problem began:
It started two days ago.
Understanding instructions:
Take it three times a day after meals.

Tell the students to copy down the examples. Assign any review homework you feel is necessary. Tell the class that in the next lesson, they will learn how to invite people out.

Ask the class to read the *Background notes* for Unit 8 before the next class.

Optional Activity

Review: word puzzle

Books closed. Write the following words with missing letters on the board and tell students that they used these words in Unit 7. Ask them to guess what the words are.

The first student to finish is the winner!

1 _ o _ t _ r
2 t _ r r _ b l _
3 p _ _ n f _ l
4 t _ i _ e
5 _ r e _ c r _ p _ i _ n
6 c _ _ d
7 h u _ _ _ n g
8 _ e v e _

Answers:

1 doctor
2 terrible
3 painful
4 twice
5 prescription
6 cold
7 hurting
8 fever

Unit 8
Are you free this weekend?

Topic / functions

Making invitations

Accepting and refusing invitations politely

Rescheduling invitations

Review

At the doctor's

Write the following chain dialog on the board. Put students in pairs and give an example for the first box. Students should not write the conversation but use the boxes as prompts to create a spoken dialog. At the end of the activity, nominate a few students and listen to their conversations.

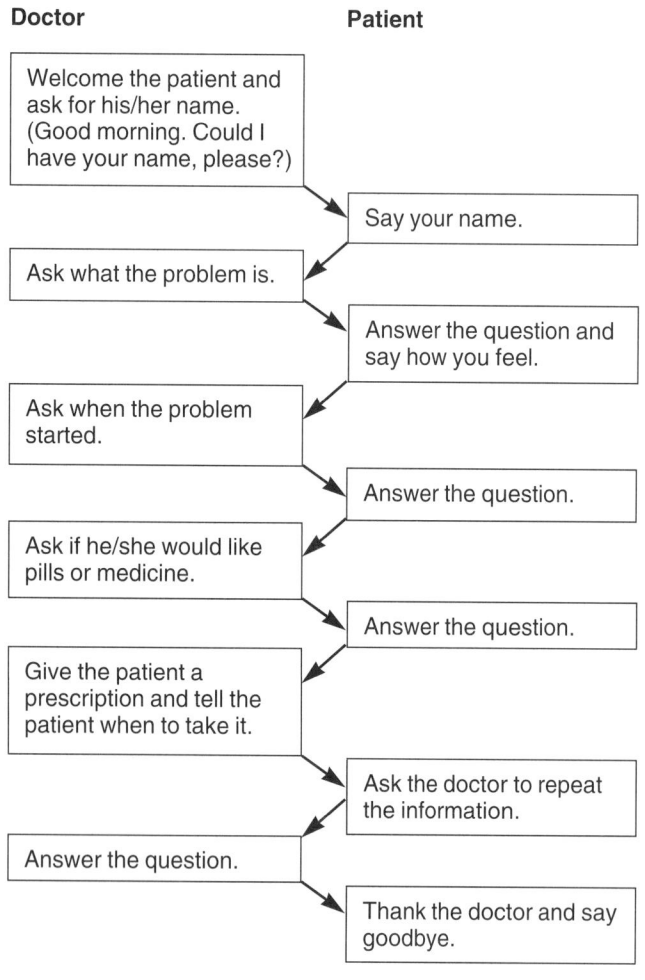

Doctor | **Patient**

Welcome the patient and ask for his/her name. (Good morning. Could I have your name, please?)

Say your name.

Ask what the problem is.

Answer the question and say how you feel.

Ask when the problem started.

Answer the question.

Ask if he/she would like pills or medicine.

Answer the question.

Give the patient a prescription and tell the patient when to take it.

Ask the doctor to repeat the information.

Answer the question.

Thank the doctor and say goodbye.

Warming up

Preview: Background notes for Unit 8

Books closed. Brainstorm places that your students would take a foreign visitor to in Japan and list them on the board, e.g., Food and drink – to a restaurant, bar, izakaya pub, hotel, etc. Entertainment – to the theater, sightseeing, shopping, etc.

If the class level is high, ask some general questions and point out any cultural differences, e.g.:

Would you ask a visitor to your home?
What time would you ask them to arrive?
What time would you expect them to arrive?

Tell the students that in this unit, Makoto is going to meet his British friend, John.

Open your books

Tell the students to look at the picture on p. 22 of their books. Read the caption aloud: *John Taylor is arranging to have lunch with Makoto.*

Listening

Read the instructions aloud. Some of your class may be weak at telling the time. However, they should be able to complete the task receptively, even if they are less confident about telling the time productively. For weak groups, at some point in the lesson make sure that you use the *Optional Activity: Telling time* below.

Students who are unable to spell the days of the week should use the pocket diary artwork for reference.

When everyone is ready, play the cassette through once without stopping. Lower-level classes may have difficulties the first time through due to the amount of information. Reassure students that they will hear the conversations several times and not to panic! After the first time, tell the students to check their answers in pairs.

Play the cassette again, this time pausing after each dialog. If they are struggling, replay the key sentences (e.g., *The Gorham on Wednesday at 7:30.*) and pause the tape after playing each one.

Play the tape one more time through without stopping. Have the students check answers in pairs. Elicit the answers and write them on the board. Remind the class to check their spelling of the days and ask if the times refer to the morning, afternoon, or night. Add A.M. or P.M. to the times.

Answers:
1 Wednesday, 7:30 P.M.
2 Friday, 6:00 P.M.
3 Saturday, 10:00 A.M.

Optional Activity

Telling time

For groups which are unable to tell time, spend a few minutes teaching basic time-telling, using a model clock and moving the hands or by drawing the times on the board. Write the following times on the board: 3:00, 3:05, 3:10, 3:15, 3:20, 3:25, 3:30, 3:35, 3:40, 3:45, 3:50, 3:55, 4:00.

Teach the class the simplest way to read these times (*three o'clock, three oh five, three ten, three fifteen, three twenty*, etc.).

Ask individual students some questions to elicit times, e.g., *What time do you get up? / go to bed? / eat breakfast?* and have them practice in pairs. If the group is coping well and your schedule allows, spend some more time teaching alternative ways of time-telling: *a quarter after three / half past three / a quarter to four*, etc.

Higher-level groups may be taught the twenty-four-hour clock, which is useful for itineraries and tour schedules. However, students should be able to cope if they are comfortable using only the first way of telling the time as suggested above, so do not feel compelled to push your group to learn all the ways at once.

Look and learn

Books closed. Drill the questions and answers. Draw three pictures on the board of a smiling face, a serious face, and a frowning face, to represent *Yes*, *Maybe*, and *No*.

Yes   Maybe   No

Explain the first three answers in *Look and learn* by pointing to these pictures, and after practicing, use the pictures to elicit responses from the students, e.g.:

T: *Are you free for dinner on Monday, Yasuko?*
   (points to frowning face)

S: *Oh, sorry. I'm afraid I'm busy then.*

T: *Can you make it for dinner on Tuesday, Eiichi?*
   (points to serious face)

S: *I can't make it Tuesday, but how about Wednesday?*

T: *Yes, that's fine.*

T: *Are you free for lunch tomorrow, Yukimi?*
   (points to smiling face)

S: *That sounds great. I'd love to.*

Model the intonation patterns for these questions and answers carefully, so that the students sound appropriately enthusiastic or regretful when they respond.

After practicing all the target language, students open their books to p. 22 and practice in pairs.

Optional Activity

Extra information

Higher-level classes can be told to add to the information in the Look and learn using the present continuous tense to talk about future plans, e.g., *Oh, sorry. I'm busy then. I'm going shopping with my friends / meeting Toshiko / seeing a movie / playing volleyball / watching a ball game.*

Be aware, however, that this area is covered in depth later in the course (Unit 13, which deals with explaining one's plans for the day).

Teach some other ways to ask people out:

Would you like to see a movie / have dinner with me on Tuesday?

For vocabulary extension, put students in pairs to brainstorm "things to do" under the headings: *Food and drink*, *Live performances*, *Sports*, and *With friends*, e.g.:

Food and drink	**Sports**
go to a restaurant	watch a ball game
meet for coffee	play volleyball
have a picnic	go skiing
Live performances	**With friends**
see a movie	go to a party
go to a concert	go to a barbecue
go to the theater	visit Seiko

Elicit answers and write them on the board. Give the class time to copy down the lists.

Have the students practice the *Look and learn* in pairs, but using their own information and some of the examples above. Ask them to imagine that they are meeting a foreign friend here in Japan. Elicit some common meeting places (e.g., In Tokyo: in front of Hachiko; in front of Studio Alta; at the police box at … station; at the north/south/east/west ticket gate of … station; in front of … department store; in the … Hotel lobby). This helps to remind students that meeting places need to be quite specific and encourages them to use as much language as possible when practicing.

Conversation

Hold your book so that the students can see p. 23. Say: *Look at page 23. Look at the "Conversation."* Read the instructions aloud and check that everyone is ready to start. Play the tape through once without stopping. Let the students check answers in pairs. Play the tape again, this time pausing after each blank, and replaying any parts that the students have trouble hearing. Play the conversation through one more time without stopping and let the students check together again.

Elicit the answers and write them on the board.

Answers:
1 meet for lunch today
2 Thursday
3 12:30
4 at my hotel

Explain that *I was just wondering* means *I was thinking about something*. There should be few other problems with the conversation.

Books closed. Model the conversation, or use the cassette, to drill in chorus. After sufficient practice, ask the students to open their books and practice in pairs. Have them sit back-to-back if possible, to simulate a telephone conversation.

Confident pairs should take turns to play the part of Makoto with their books shut, responding to John as best they can, and asking for repetitions if needed.

Over to you!

Read the instructions aloud and put the students in new pairs to practice. Ask them to sit back-to-back if possible. Monitor from a distance for pronunciation problems and give feedback at the end of the exercise. Have some pairs act out their dialogs for the rest of the class. By this stage in the course, students should be more comfortable with presenting their efforts to the rest of the group, but if you have a large class, bear in mind that this type of feedback can be very intimidating, and it is probably better therefore to have several pairs perform simultaneously.

Optional Activity

Dialogue ordering

Make one copy of photocopiable page H (p. 87) for each pair of students in the class and cut the pages into strips. Shuffle each set and hand out one set to each pair. Alternatively, if you prefer to have a writing stage in your class, write the dialog, mixed up, on the board. Students work in pairs to put the conversation into the correct order. Elicit the answers and have the students practice the dialog in pairs.

Activity

Ask if anyone in the class has been to San Francisco. Ask: *What did you do there? Why did you go there? Which famous places did you visit?* If no one has been there, elicit any information that the class knows about the city. If possible, bring in a map of the U.S. to show where the city is. If you have any pictures, brochures, or maps of San Francisco, use these to tell the students about the city. Drill the place names in the book.

Read the instructions aloud. Put students in new pairs and have them create their own conversations.

Monitor, and give feedback on any serious mistakes at the end of the exercise. Confident students can perform their dialogs to the rest of the class.

Optional Activities

My city/area: teacher talk

Students are usually very interested to hear about their teacher's hometown. Bring in as much realia as you can: promotional videos, pamphlets, maps, postcards, photographs, etc. Spend a few minutes giving the class general information about your area (if possible, comparing it to places in Japan so that the class can understand more easily): e.g., population, size, famous things to see, best time of year to visit.

Good classes should be able to ask questions about your town, but do not expect most students at this level to be able to form questions easily. After talking about your area, write some of the most famous places to visit on the board and show pictures if possible.

Put students in pairs and repeat the *Activity*, this time asking students to imagine that they are having a day out in your area. Monitor and conduct feedback as in the *Activity* above.

Alternatively, if your whole class is going to one particular destination, try to bring in information about that place and set up the role-play referring to tourist spots there.

The diary game

Copy photocopiable page I (p. 88) and give one diary page to each student. Tell the students to write five things (real or imagined) that they are doing next week. You may need to put some examples on the board to get them started, e.g., *do my homework, go to karaoke with my friends, do my part-time job, go skiing*, etc.

Group work. Tell the students that they have ten minutes to "telephone" as many people in the class as possible to arrange to go out with them. They must arrange a day, time, and place to meet, and write it onto their page, e.g.:

> *Tuesday: 6 P.M., Kichijoji Station West Exit.*
> *Go to dinner with Seiko.*

Do an example with a student before starting the game.

Give the class a time limit: lower-level groups will take longer to form conversations, so use your knowledge of the class to set an appropriate time limit. Monitor from a distance and especially listen in to see if the class manages to accept, refuse, and reschedule the invitations politely. Those groups which used the *Optional Activity: Extra information* above should be reminded to use the present continuous tense when making excuses, e.g., *I'm sorry, I'm playing volleyball on Wednesday. How about Thursday?*

Finishing the lesson

Bring the class back together and congratulate them for their hard work. Tell the students to look again at the Background notes for Unit 8. List the functions on the board and elicit an example for each one. Write the examples up too, e.g.:

Making invitations:
   Would you like to meet for lunch?

Accepting and refusing invitations politely:
   I'd love to. / Sorry, I'm afraid I'm busy then.

Rescheduling invitations:
   I can't make it Monday, but how about Friday?

Ask the class to copy down the examples. Assign any review homework you feel is necessary. Tell the class that in the next lesson, they will learn how to order food in a restaurant.

Ask the class to read the *Background notes* for Unit 9 before the next class.

Optional Activity

Review: invitations – missing words

Write the sentences with blanks and the "missing words" box on the board. Ask students to copy them down and fill in the blanks from the box. Tell them to check answers in pairs at the end of the exercise, and then to practice the conversation. (The sentences are given here with the answers in place.)

sounds	time	busy
at	see	about
sorry	free	how
make	Keiko	

A: Are you <u>free</u> for lunch on Saturday, Keiko?

B: That <u>sounds</u> great! Oh, no, just a minute. I'm <u>sorry</u>. I'm afraid I'm <u>busy</u> then. <u>How</u> about Sunday?

A: Yes, I can <u>make</u> it Sunday.

B: OK. What <u>time</u> should we meet?

A: How <u>about</u> 11:30 A.M.?

B: Fine. Shall we meet <u>at</u> the Garden Café?

A: That's fine. All right. <u>See</u> you then!

Unit 9
Are you ready to order?

Topic / functions
Ordering items from a menu
Asking about dishes
Asking for things in a restaurant

Review

Invitations

Make copies of photocopiable page J (p. 89), one for each student. The whole class plays, inviting their classmates out according to the information in the bubbles. Remind students to fix a time and meeting place. In order to give practice in refusing and rescheduling, ask students to use their real-life schedules. If they are busy, they should refuse or try to arrange an alternative time.

Do an example first with a confident student; if you manage to fix an appointment, demonstrate that the student's name is written in the bubble. If he or she is busy, ask another student.

Assign an appropriate time limit for the activity and monitor from a distance. At the end of the activity, ask some general questions to round off the game, e.g.:

What are you doing on Friday, Masaya?
Who are you going to the movies with, Hiromi?
Where are you going to go for lunch today, Urara?

Warming up

Preview: Background notes for Unit 9

Books closed. Remind the students about the background reading they did for Unit 9. Put students in groups of three. Tell them to list as many different kinds of food as they can think of, from as many different countries as possible (e.g., Italian food – pizza, spaghetti, macaroni; North American food – hamburgers, steak, french fries).

Help them along by suggesting other country names from time to time (e.g., Turkey, China, India, Spain, Thailand). Put a world map up on the board if you have one. This is a useful brainstorming game that tunes students in to the topic of foreign food, but is also very reassuring as students often realize that they have in fact probably tried quite a wide range of foreign food in their lives. Curries and pizza/pasta dishes, for instance, are very popular in Japan. One of the biggest worries for first-time overseas travelers is whether or not they'll like the food, and if they'll be able to cope in restaurants and with their homestay families.

Tell the students that in this unit, they will learn how to understand menus and order food in a restaurant.

Open your books

Tell the students to look at the picture on p. 24 of their books. Read the caption aloud: *Miki is ordering food in a restaurant.*

Listening

Read the instructions aloud. Ask if the students can remember which countries the characters are visiting. (Rie and Miki are in the States, Mayumi and Makoto are in the U.K. and Koji, here with his friend Pete, is in Australia.)

As a prediction activity, ask the students to guess which order they think matches the characters. This is a simple way to have the students read through the orders before listening to the cassette.

When everyone is ready, play the cassette through once. Tell the students: *Work in pairs. Check your answers together. Did you choose the same orders?*

Say: *Now listen again.* Replay the tape, stopping after each dialog. Ask higher-level groups to write a name next to each item on the menu to show who ordered what. Elicit the answers by asking: *What did Rie order? How about Miki?* etc., and write them on the board.

Answers:
1 c **2** a **3** b

Look and learn

Books closed. If possible, bring in an authentic, large menu as a prop. Draw simple pictures on the board of an *appetizer* (U.S. English; *starter* U.K. English), an *entrée* (main course), and a *dessert* (e.g., soup, pizza, and ice cream). Pre-teach the names for different parts of a meal and elicit examples if possible. Draw a picture of a glass of wine as well.

Drill the questions. Use the menu and pictures as prompts, e.g.:

T: (holds up menu)
SS: *Would you like to see the menu?*
T: (points to the picture of wine)
SS: *Would you like something to drink?*

Model the answers carefully to ensure that, when ordering, the students are saying *I'd like* and not *I like*; *I'll have* and not *I have*. *Certainly* was taught in Unit 1 but you may need to remind students that it means *Yes, of course*, and that the stress is on the first syllable. *The check* (U.S.) is *the bill* in British English.

After practicing all of *Look and learn*, students open their books to p. 24 and practice in pairs.

Conversation

Hold your book so that the students can see p. 25. Say: *Look at page 25. Look at the "Conversation."* Read the instructions aloud. Students should be familiar with this type of activity by now and proceed with little difficulty. Put weaker classes in pairs to complete the conversation speculatively before listening.

Play the cassette. Tell the class: *Listen to the conversation with Miki. Check the conversation. Did you get the answers right?* Let students check in pairs, and then replay the tape, pausing after each blank so that students have time to change their answers if they wish.

Play the cassette one more time through without stopping. If your class completed the task with ease, have them close their eyes as they listen to the conversation for the last time and tell them to listen carefully to try to understand as much of the conversation as possible.

Elicit the answers and write them on the board. If you have any food magazine pictures, try to bring in a picture of Black Forest Gateau to show the class. Tell the class that *Your order won't be long* means that the food will arrive soon.

Answers:

1 e **2** b **3** d **4** a **5** f **6** c

Books closed. Model the conversation, or use the cassette, to drill in chorus. After sufficient practice, students open their books to p. 25 and practice in pairs, using the "read, look up and speak" technique.

Over to you!

Read the instructions aloud and put the students in new pairs to practice. You may wish to model the pronunciation of the food names first. Monitor from a distance and offer help when asked by the students. Have confident students stand up if they are playing the part of server and act out as much as possible (taking notes of the order, clearing plates away, etc.). Nominate students to perform their role-plays for the rest of the class.

Optional Activities

Class menu

Tell the class that they have just opened a new restaurant in town. Take a vote to decide what kind of restaurant it should be (e.g., fast food, Italian). Brainstorm a menu and write it on the board, e.g.:

Class A Burger House!

Burgers:
cheeseburger, double cheeseburger, etc.
Drinks:
Milk shakes: vanilla, chocolate, strawberry
Coke, Pepsi, Tea, coffee, juice
Extras:
Onion rings, french fries, etc.

Books closed. Put students in small groups or pairs and have them improvise conversations using the menu on the board. With a higher-level class, brainstorm prices as well and write them too. If you do this, pre-teach *How much is that, please?* and *That comes to…*. This type of role-play is fun as the class feels very involved, having produced the menu themselves. Fast-food restaurants are very popular with college-age students. Give feedback at the end of the activity and congratulate students who did their best and managed to refrain from slipping back into Japanese.

Dictation and Interview activity

Dictate the following questions to the class and have them write them down in a list.

What is your favorite foreign food?

(You may need to spell out *favorite* and *foreign*. Explain *favorite* to weak groups.)

What food do you really hate?

What is your favorite restaurant in Japan?

How many times in one month do you eat out?

(Explain that *eat out* means *eat in a restaurant*.)

What is your favorite drink?

What new food would you like to try for the first time?

Have students ask you the questions to start with to give examples and to make the questions clear to everyone.

Tell the class to interview three classmates (preferably ones they don't usually work with). They should ask the questions but only write one-word or short answers.

At the end of the activity, elicit some of the more interesting answers you heard as you monitored.

Activity

Read the instructions aloud. Put students in new pairs and allocate roles. Remind students to cover the *Conversation* and *Look and learn* sections to make the activity as free as possible. Model the pronunciation of the names of the food items before the students start.

Remind students that a *vegetarian* is someone who doesn't eat meat or fish. If possible, bring in as much realia as possible to create a restaurant atmosphere. Servers can be given small notepads to take orders on; you can play quiet music in the background, etc. Confident groups should be encouraged to think about the character they are playing (a friendly/bored server? A customer in a hurry? etc.).

Give feedback on any serious errors at the end of the activity and have some students perform their dialogs for the rest of the group.

Finishing the lesson

Bring the class back together and congratulate them on their efforts. Tell the students to look again at the *Background notes* for Unit 9. List the functions on the board and elicit an example for each one. Write the examples too, e.g.:

Ordering items from a menu:
I'd like the fish, please.
Asking about dishes:
What's "linguini"?
Asking for things in a restaurant:
May I have the check, please?

Ask the class to copy down the examples. Assign any review homework you feel is necessary. Tell the class that in the next lesson, they will learn how to talk about their family. Ask the students to bring in a photo of their family next time, if they have one.

Ask students to read the *Background notes* for Unit 10 before the next class.

Optional Activity

Review: matching the questions and answers

Write the following questions and answers on the board. Ask students to copy them down and match the questions to the correct answers. They should then practice the questions and answers in pairs.

The questions:

1 Excuse me. What's *sushi*?
2 I'm sorry, Yoshiko. I don't understand this. What's *soba*?
3 Would you like something to drink?
4 Could I have an ashtray, please?
5 Are you ready to order?
6 May we have the check, please?

The answers:

a Yes, I think so.
b It's raw fish with rice, madam.
c I'm sorry, sir. This is a no-smoking restaurant.
d Certainly, madam. How will you be paying?
e They're buckwheat noodles. They taste great!
f I'll have mineral water, please.

Answers:

1 b **2** e **3** f **4** c **5** a **6** d

Unit 10
My father works in a bank

Topic / functions
Understanding questions about your family

Talking about your family

Talking about where you live

Review

In a restaurant: scrambled sentences
Write these scrambled sentences on the board and ask students to work in pairs to reorder them correctly:

1 like What dessert for you would ?
2 me what's Excuse chowder clam ?
3 ready order to you Are ?
4 steak please like the I'd
5 wine Could have glass I red a of ?

Answers:
1 What would you like for dessert?
2 Excuse me. What's clam chowder?
3 Are you ready to order?
4 I'd like the steak, please.
5 Could I have a glass of red wine?

Warming up

Preview: Background notes for Unit 10
Books closed. Remind the class about the *Background notes* they read for Unit 10. If you have a reasonably good class, start to draw your family tree on the board and have the students ask questions about your family as you draw the tree, in order to brainstorm "family members" vocabulary (*Do you have a sister? What's her name?* etc.).

Higher-level classes should be able to tell you from the *Background notes* which topic areas are not normally discussed when meeting people for the first time (age, weight, salary, religious beliefs). For weaker groups, bring in a photo of your family and tell the group a little about them, and list any new vocabulary on the board. Most classes should be able to cope with *father*, *mother*, *sister*, and *brother*, but you may need to pre-teach words such as *older brother*, *younger sister*, *only child*, *parents*, *grandparents*, *cousin*, and so on.

Open your books
Tell the students to look at the picture on p. 26. Read the unit title. Remind the students that Miki and Rie have a friend in the States called Amy. Read the caption aloud: *Miki and Rie are talking to their friend, Amy*.

Listening
Read through the instructions. The students should be familiar with true/false questions by now. Read the sentences aloud. When everyone is ready, play the cassette and monitor to check that everyone is completing the task. Tell the students to work in pairs and check their answers together.

Replay the cassette, pausing after each dialog. If the class is having difficulties, replay the key sentences (e.g., *He works in a bank.*) and pause after playing them.

Tell the students to check again together and elicit the answers by taking a class vote. If necessary replay the relevant part, pause the tape, and repeat the sentence slowly yourself. Write the answers on the board.

Answers:
1 T   2 F   3 F   4 T   5 T

Higher-level classes may benefit from looking over the tapescript of one or two of these short conversations. Explain *suburb* and *born to shop* if you use the tapescript for additional practice.

Look and learn
Books closed. Model the questions and answers clearly but at normal speed and with natural intonation. Students should remember *What do you do?* from Unit 1 and be able to deduce that *What does you father do?* means *What is his job?* However, explain again if necessary. For weaker classes, explain *usually* by drawing a frequency line on the board (*never*, *not often*, *not usually*, *sometimes*, *usually*, *often*, *always*) and giving examples.

After sufficient practice drilling the questions and answers, students open their books to p. 26 and practice in pairs. After practicing, one person in each pair should close their book as his or her partner asks the questions again. This time, the students should use real information about their families. Note that explaining what their parents do for a living can be very difficult and you may wish to encourage use of bilingual dictionaries at this point.

Teach the structure *My mother works in ...* (company name) and explain that *salaryman*, which students frequently use, is Japanese English and not used by native speakers. The equivalent is *businessman*. Higher-level groups may be able to explain what kind of work their parents do by giving examples (e.g., *My mother works in a travel agency. She arranges trips in Japan for older people.*) but do not expect most students at false-beginner level to be able to explain their answers. If your class level is high, you may wish to spend some time teaching occupation-related vocabulary, e.g., *freelance, self-employed, branch, part-time, full-time, overtime.*

Conversation

Hold your books so that the students can see p. 27. Say: *Look at page 27. Look at the "Conversation."* Read the instructions aloud. If the class is weak, read through the conversation before playing the cassette and pre-teach *suburbs.*

Point again to the picture on p. 26 of Rie showing Amy a photo of her family and talking about her family. Check that everyone is ready to start, and play the cassette. Monitor to check that everyone is completing the task. Have the students check in pairs and then replay the tape, this time pausing after each blank, to give the class time to change their answers if they wish. Play the conversation through one more time without stopping. Elicit the answers and write them on the board so that the students can check their spelling.

> *Answers*:
> 1 42
> 2 for Sony
> 3 schoolteacher
> 4 one brother and one sister
> 5 small apartment
> 6 play tennis

Books closed. Model the conversation, or use the cassette, to drill in chorus. Students may have problems with the intonation in the answer to *Do you have any brothers or sisters? Yes, I have **one** brother and **one** sister.* They may also find the vowel sound in *suburbs* difficult. After practicing, have the students open their books again to p. 27 and try out the conversation in pairs, using the "read, look up and speak" technique. Monitor and offer help and corrections as necessary.

Over to you!

New pairs. The students should be comfortable with this type of activity by now. With higher-level groups, tell them to cover the *Conversation* and to use the prompts alone to make a new dialog. Listen out for any pronunciation problems and drill the correct intonation patterns as necessary. Nominate some students to perform their conversations for the rest of the class.

Optional Activities

About families: true or false?

Write three sentences on the board about your family, house, or hobbies, similar to the things that Rie says about her family. Two of the sentences should be true, but one should be untrue, e.g.:

1 I have three sisters, and I'm the youngest in our family.
2 My father works for a building company, and my mother is a teacher.
3 On the weekends, I like to go hiking with my friends and sometimes I play ice hockey.

Ask the students to guess which sentence is false. Take a class vote.

Then ask the class to write down three sentences about themselves (two true and one false). Monitor the writing stage, and be available to offer help and corrections as necessary.

Put the students in small groups of about four, preferably with classmates they do not know very well. Students read their sentences aloud and the other members guess which sentence is incorrect.

Beanbag circle: fast interviews!

Books closed. Ask the students to sit in a circle. Six to eight students is a good number for this exercise. Give each group a beanbag or ball. Tell the students that the object of the game is to keep the beanbag moving as much as possible. Tell the students to ask questions about families, homes, and hobbies (as in the *Look and learn* section). When they ask a question, they should make eye contact with another student and throw the beanbag. The catcher answers the question as fast as possible and asks another question, throwing the beanbag to the new respondent. This is a simple question and answer activity, but the beanbag-throwing element adds speed to the game and encourages learners to make their questions quickly and their replies instant (something that false beginners can find very hard to do). If your group is weak, you may wish to put some prompts on the board to help (e.g., *Hobby? Father? Sister? Weekend? Live?*).

The idea behind the game can be reversed if you tell the class that they must try to hold onto the beanbag as long as possible. When they are asked a question, they should try to give as lengthy a reply as possible, but without pausing or repeating themselves, and only making a new question when they have run out of things to say. (This is not as much fun as fast-throwing activities, however!)

Activity

New partners. If you asked your students to bring in photos of their families, ask them to use them during this activity. If not, students should spend a few minutes drawing a simple picture of their families in the box given on p. 27. Some learners will want to produce masterpieces, so if your lesson is drawing to a close, set a time limit for the picture-drawing phase (and ban the use of erasers to speed things up if necessary!).

Put students in groups of three to talk about their pictures or photos. The temptation to use the mother tongue can be very high in this activity, so you may want to ask students to keep a check on themselves. Every time they say something in Japanese, they should make a mark on a piece of note paper to keep a tally of the number of times their concentration slips. Merely by asking students to keep a watch on themselves tends to keep the number down. (Do not turn this into any kind of score sheet, though. It is better **not** to ask students to tell you how many marks they made at the end.)

Make sure that students cover the words in Unit 10 as they do the activity and encourage them to use as much English as they can during this free-practice phase. Monitor from a distance and give feedback at the end of the activity on any serious frequently-made mistakes.

Finishing the lesson

Bring the class back together and congratulate them for their efforts. If any students have brought in amusing photos (for instance, students will often bring in pictures of their pets as well, when asked to bring in pictures of their family), you could ask the students to show their classmates. You could also ask some general feedback questions to various students. Be sensitive to any students who do not wish to discuss certain points about their backgrounds, particularly in the case of deaths and divorces, and other sensitive areas. This reinforces the importance of careful monitoring while an activity is going on!

Tell the students to look again at the *Background notes* for Unit 10. List the functions on the board and elicit an example for each one. Write the examples too, e.g.:

Understanding questions about your family:
Do you have any brothers or sisters?
Talking about your family:
My father works in a bank.
Talking about where you live:
I live in an apartment in Tokyo.

Tell the students to copy down the examples. Assign any review homework you feel is necessary. If you are planning to go straight onto Unit 11 next time, tell the students that they will learn how to answer questions and talk about Japan. Ask the class to read the

Background notes to Unit 11 before the next lesson. If you are going to spend a whole lesson on the second *Out and About* page, leave the *Background notes* reading until next time.

Optional Activity

Review: family questionnaire

Put students in small groups of four or five. Tell the students that they are going to conduct a class survey about homes, family, and hobbies. In groups, have the students write five or six questions that they want to know about their classmates. You may need to do some examples to show the class different types of questions they might want to use, e.g.:

True or false?
  My father usually works on Saturdays.   *T   F*
Multiple choice. Choose one answer:
  a *I have never been skiing.*
  b *I have been skiing once or twice.*
  c *I have been skiing three or four times in my life.*
  d *I have been skiing many times.*
Yes/No questions:
  Do your grandparents live with you?
Questions which need a short answer:
  How many people are there in your family?

Monitor the question-writing phase carefully and offer help and suggestions as necessary.

Once the students have written their questions in their groups, re-group the class so that one person from each original group is in each new group. The students then ask and answer questions and note down the answers of each person in the new group.

Ask the students to return to their original groups and pool their answers. Hand out large sheets of paper and have the students record the results of their surveys in graphic form (e.g., pie chart, bar graph, interesting facts-style poster). Put the finished products on the wall.

Out and About 2
Eating Out

Read through the notes in the introduction on p. 7 first, for additional ideas on how to use the *Out and About* pages.

This unit is concerned with the language that often goes untaught when teaching learners how to order food in cafés or restaurants. Spend a few minutes brainstorming with the class the different places to buy food when in a foreign country. Remind the class that convenience stores and supermarkets sell sandwiches and other snacks for lunchtime and that there are fast-food restaurants everywhere, as in Japan. In addition, just as Japan has, for example, *yaki-imo* (sweet potato) vans and food stalls on the streets in many cities, so do other countries have their equivalents (e.g., hamburger or kebab vans, hot dog stands, ice cream vendors).

Look at the pictures on pp. 28–29. Ask: *What do you think they are going to eat? Where are they?*

Answers:

● Koji is in an open-air street café in Sydney. Tell the students that the café culture is very popular with young people in Australia. Koji is having a cup of coffee.

● Makoto and Mayumi are buying ice-cream cones from an ice-cream van in the U.K. Soft drinks are also sold in these vans, usually found at beaches and tourist spots, although some towns also have vans that drive around the streets in the summer selling icecream. Teach *soft drink*.

● Miki and Rie are in a restaurant in the U.S. We don't know what they are going to eat.

● Miki and Rie are in a fast-food restaurant in the U.S. Brainstorm some typical fast foods with the class (e.g., *french fries*, *burgers*, *shakes*, *fried chicken*) that the girls might buy.

● Koji is in an Australian seafood restaurant. Names of different kinds of fish can be very difficult for students to learn. You may wish to spend a few minutes building up a class menu on the board of different kinds of fish and fish dishes that your students may want to eat overseas. Teach words such as *lobster* and *crab* too.

● Mayumi and Makoto are in a pub in the U.K. (with their English friend, John) eating food in the pub garden. Remind the class that pubs abroad are quite different from Japanese *izakayas*. There is no server, and you have to go to the bar yourself to order and collect your drinks. However, many pubs now serve food, especially at lunchtime.

Have the students read the conversations. Explain any difficult vocabulary, e.g.:

another	one more; a second (or third, etc.) cup of coffee. Remind students to check whether the café has a refill service or if they will have to pay for another cup.
black	without milk or cream
white	with milk or cream
Please wait to be seated	you must stand next to the sign until a server tells you where to sit.
to stay	to eat in the restaurant
to go	to take the food away
slurp	the sound you make when you eat noodles, for example. Makoto doesn't realize that it isn't polite to slurp food in many Western cultures, and Mayumi is shocked by her husband. *Excuse me* or *I'm sorry* is the appropriate apology in this case. You may wish to spend a few minutes on table manners in different countries and what to say if you make a mistake.

Model the mini-dialogs and drill as necessary. Have the students practice in pairs, and listen to some of them at the end of the activity. Better classes may be able to lengthen the dialogs by adding more information (e.g., Koji might ask for the check; Makoto might ask for some change for a five-pound note). Remind weaker groups to record any useful new phrases in their vocabulary books.

Write five or six more "eating out" situations on the board, e.g. asking for a glass of water, buying a burger without onions, asking for a seat near the window, asking what time "last orders" are, checking if you can pay by credit card, asking for another cup of tea.

Put the students into small groups and tell them to write and practice mini-dialogs for one or two of the situations. Monitor and offer help as necessary. Have some groups perform their role-plays for the rest of the class at the end of the activity. Give feedback at the end.

Unit 11
What's your favorite food?

Topic / functions
Talking about Japan
Answering questions about Japan
Disagreeing politely

Review

Drawing game

Look at p. 26 for the instructions on how to play a vocabulary-review drawing game. Use these words from Unit 10:

family	apartment	station
photograph	hobby	businessman
suburb	parents	only child
housewife	older sister	weekend

Optional Activity

Review: units 1–10

If your scheduling allows, you may wish to spend some time reviewing vocabulary from the previous units at the start of this lesson, being halfway through the course at this point. The drawing game is a fun way to review, but you may find that spelling tests or class quizzes are just as effective. Use your knowledge of the class to assign appropriate review homework. It is usually very good for class morale when they realize how much material they have covered during the course so far!

Photocopiable page K (p.90) is a simple board game to be played in groups of three or four students. Enlarge the page and make one copy for each group. Hand out dice and counters. Students throw the dice and move their counters around the board. The questions have all been taught in Units 1–10 and students should answer as best they can. The numbers on the board refer to the units in which the questions appeared.

If they land on a "free question" square, they should ask the person on their left any question in English. Your role as teacher while the game is in progress is to monitor, offer help and corrections, and make a note of any points that need reviewing with the whole class later.

Warming up

Preview: Background notes for Unit 11

Books closed. Remind the class about the *Background notes* they read for Unit 11. Tell the students what some of your impressions of Japan and Japanese people were before you started teaching them or before you came to Japan. If possible, bring in a number of Japanese objects or pictures of typically Japanese things to use during the lesson (e.g., a map of Japan, chopsticks, a book in Japanese; pictures of cherry blossoms, Mount Fuji, the *shinkansen* (bullet train), a Japanese-style house, the Prime Minister).

Open your books

Tell the class that when they make new friends abroad, they will need to be ready to talk about Japan. Ask the students to look at p. 30. Remind the class that Koji is on a Working Holiday Visa in Sydney, Australia, and that he is staying with a homestay family for two or three months to get to know a real Australian family and to improve his English. Remind the class that Mr. and Mrs. Todd are his homestay "parents" (we first saw them in Unit 6, when Koji was asking how to use things around the house).

Read the caption aloud: *Koji is talking to the Todds about Japan.*

Listening

Read the instructions aloud and read through the four sentences. Explain *white mask*, *pollution*, and *raw fish* if necessary. Check that the students understand that these are the Todds' ideas about Japan. Ask: *Does Koji tell them their ideas are right or wrong?*

When everyone is ready, play the cassette. Tell the students: *Work in pairs. Check your answers together. Did you circle the same answers?*

Say: *Now listen again.* Replay the cassette, stopping after each dialog to give the students a chance to change their answers if they wish. If they are struggling, replay the key sentences (e.g., *Not really. In fact, Japanese and Chinese are very different.*) and pause after playing them.

Tell the class to check in pairs again and elicit the answers by taking a class vote. Write the answers on the board.

Answers:
1 No 2 Yes 3 No 4 No

Look and learn

Books closed. Ask the class questions to see if they can guess any of the statistics given in the language study (e.g., *What's the population of Japan? What percentage of people do you think live in cities?*). Give a range of answers for students to choose from and take a class vote if individuals are unwilling to hazard a guess.

Then have the students open their books to p. 30 to look at the facts given. Some of the vocabulary is complex for false beginners, so spend time making sure that the class can understand the information. Explain *import*, *export*, and *timber*. Model the sentences, pointing to the pictures representing each fact. Tell the students to practice repeating the information in pairs.

Drill the language box showing ways of disagreeing politely. Explain that these ways are much more polite than a direct *No*. Write the sentences on the board and mark the intonation above the sentences to show how we use our voices to be polite:

Actually, it's very different.

Not really. In fact, it's very different.

Read the instructions under the language box and have the students practice pointing to the pictures and recalling the information. Monitor to see if they manage to correct each other politely. If there are problems, replay one or two of the initial listening dialogs to show how Koji corrects the Todds politely.

Optional Activity

That's not right!

Write some patently false facts and/or definitions about things Japanese on the board. Tell the class to work in pairs and take turns to read out the information. Their partner should correct them as politely as possible. For example:

1 Mount Fuji is in Tokyo.
2 The Prime Minister of Japan is Mr. Hosokawa, isn't he?
3 Japan exports a lot of oil.
4 Most Japanese people are vegetarians.

Inventive groups should be able to create their own examples too.

Conversation

Hold your book so that the students can see p. 31. Say: *Look at page 31. Look at the "Conversation."* Read the instructions aloud and give the students time to complete the conversation speculatively before listening to the tape.

Play the tape and let the students check their answers in pairs. If they have difficulties, replay the conversation, pausing after each blank to give them a chance to change their answers.

Play the conversation through one more time without stopping. Elicit the answers and write them on the board.

Answers:
1 a **2** c **3** d **4** b **5** e

Books closed. Model the conversation, or use the cassette, drilling chorally. Practice again the polite intonation patterns we use when disagreeing with someone. After drilling the whole conversation, have the students open their books again and practice in pairs. Higher-level groups should be able to substitute different kinds of Japanese food, such as *shabu-shabu* and *soba*, into the conversation. Write a list on the board as prompts.

Over to you!

New pairs. Read the instructions and have the students practice the two new dialogs. Pre-teach *martial art*; you may also need to explain that cricket is a popular summer sport in Britain. Monitor and give general feedback at the end of the exercise. Nominate some students to perform their dialogs for the rest of the group.

Optional Activity

Interview the teacher or guest speaker

Higher-level classes can be stretched in this unit by making copies of photocopiable page L (p. 91). If your establishment allows, the best way to use this sheet is to invite a guest or guests into your classroom for the learners to interview. The visitors can use the same sheet to interview the students about Japan. Prepare the students for the visit by having them ask you questions about your home country first.

If you are unable to have visitors come to your class, let the students use the sheets to interview you, or have them complete as much of the sheet as they can for homework. This is very useful if the students will be traveling overseas shortly, as it encourages research into the country they are to visit.

Photocopiable page X can be simplified for lower-level groups by reducing the number of squares to fill in, or by providing all the questions that need to be asked. For example:

Which animals are the most common in your country? /
What is the most popular pet in your country?
Which religions are most common in your country? /
Is there a state religion in your country?
Which is the wettest month in your country? /
Does your country have a rainy season?
Tell me about typical food in your country. /
What do you usually eat for dinner?

Alternatively, give one sheet to each pair and have the students take turns to ask their partner about the topics on the sheet. The speaker should talk about Japan.

Activity

New partners. Read the instructions aloud. Allocate roles. Tell the students to try to use as much English as possible in the Activity. Some of the questions are quite demanding, but the students should do their best to give some sort of answer in each case.

If your group is quite weak, you may prefer to put the students in groups of three. One student plays part A but two students together play part B to produce a joint answer.

Monitor from a distance to see how well the students can cope with unexpected questions and if they can respond politely.

At the end of the exercise, nominate several students to repeat their "best" questions and answers: you may want to write some of the good responses on the board for the class to copy down.

Give feedback on any general mistakes and have the class correct them.

Finishing the lesson

Bring the class together and congratulate them on their efforts. Tell the class to look again at the *Background notes* for Unit 11. List the functions on the board and elicit an example for each one. Write the examples too, e.g.:

Talking about Japan:
About 80% of the population live in cities.
Answering questions about Japan:
What does Japan import?
Japan imports oil, timber, and food.
Disagreeing politely:
Is Japanese similar to Chinese?
Not really. In fact, it's quite different.

Ask the class to copy down the examples. Assign any review homework you feel is necessary. Tell the class that in the next lesson, they will learn how to talk about experiences and ask for opinions.

Ask the students to read the *Background notes* for Unit 12 before the next class.

Optional Activity

Review: matching the questions and answers

Write the following questions and answers on the board. Ask students to copy them down and match the questions to the correct answer. They should then practice the questions and answers in pairs.

The questions:

1 How many people are there in Japan?
2 What do Japanese people wear?
3 What's Japan's national sport?
4 Do you celebrate Christmas?
5 What's the population of Tokyo?
6 What's the best place to go sightseeing?
7 What's your favorite food?

The answers:

a Not really. The stores sell Christmas goods, but the New Year is the traditional holiday. We eat special New Year food and some people go to the temple. It's a national holiday, and stores, banks, and offices are shut.

b We wear clothes just like you. People sometimes wear *kimono* but only for really special times, like weddings or graduation ceremonies. I always wear jeans to college!

c I think the population of the country is about 123 million people. How about your country?

d Oh, it's *sumo* wrestling. But actually, soccer, golf, baseball, and volleyball are popular too. I like playing tennis. I've never seen *sumo*.

e I like *udon*. It's a kind of soup with thick noodles, and it's really delicious. Have you tried any Japanese food?

f Oh, it's huge. About 12 million, some people say. Other people say it's much more!

g I like Kyoto best. It's a very traditional Japanese city with hundreds of temples and shrines. And it's beautiful when the cherry blossoms are out!

Answers:

1 c **2** b **3** d **4** a **5** f **6** g **7** e

Unit 12
What would you like to drink?

Topic / functions

Offering someone a drink

Asking people about their opinions

Asking and answering about experiences

Review

Facts about Japan

Books closed. Draw on the board the icons next to *Look and learn* on p. 30 of the Student Book. Tell the students to work in pairs. They should try to remember some facts about Japan, using the artwork as a prompt. If their partner remembers differently, he/she should correct the other person.

Nominate students around the class to tell you the answers and review any weak areas as necessary.

Warming up

Preview: Background notes for Unit 12

Books closed. Remind the class about the *Background notes* they read for Unit 12. Ask the students how old you must be to drink alcohol in Japan, Australia, the U.S. and the U.K. Have the class tell you some differences between pubs and *izakayas*. If any of your class have been abroad, ask them where they went to meet the local people (e.g., cafés, restaurants, discos, sports clubs, parties).

Tell the class that when they meet the local people in a country, they will often be asked what they have done in that country, where they have been, and if they enjoyed themselves.

Open your books

Ask the students to look at p. 32 of their books. Remind the class that Makoto is in the U.K. and that he has a British friend, John Taylor. (We first met John in Unit 8, when he invited Makoto out for lunch.) Tell the class that the picture shows a typical English pub and ask the students what they can see in the picture. Read the caption aloud: *Makoto is in a pub with John.*

Listening

Tell the class that they will hear conversations where Koji, Rie, and Miki are meeting people. Read the instructions and the sentences aloud. Pre-teach *schooner* and *alligator*. When everyone is ready, play the cassette. Tell the students: *Work in pairs. Check your answers. Did you circle the same things?*

Say: *Now listen again.* Replay the cassette, stopping after each question. If the class is struggling, replay the key sentences (e.g., *That's four dollars twenty cents, please.*) and pause after playing them. Play the conversations through one more time and let the students check their answers together. Elicit the answers by taking a class vote, and write them on the board.

Answers:
1 T 2 F 3 T (flowers) 4 F

Look and learn

Books closed. Drill the questions and answers. Draw smiling and frowning faces on the board and use them to elicit positive or negative responses to the questions. Explain *frogs' legs*, *awful*, and *What was it like?*

After sufficient practice, have the students practice in pairs with their books open. Higher-level classes may be able to substitute other adjectives into their answers. Tell the students to imagine that their partner is a foreign tourist to Japan. They should ask questions about sightseeing in Japan and Japanese food (*Have you been to Nara yet? Have you eaten sushi?* etc.). This usually elicits a wider range of answers. If students start using their own questions, listen for the common mistake *Have you ever…? * Yes, I have ever…* and correct immediately!

Optional Activity

Past participles

False-beginner level students will be able to remember a surprisingly large number of past participles. To prepare them for using the present perfect in this unit, it is a good idea for students to review what they already know. Have them work in pairs. Tell them that they are going to test each other on verbs they learned in school. (Students are usually taught these structures like this: *eat–ate–eaten.*) Copy photocopiable pages M and N (pp. 92-93) and cut up to make verb cards. Hand out one card to each student. Student A reads out the infinitive form of the verb on his/her card to Student B; Student B responds by telling Student A the past tense and past participle. Do an example first yourself to make this clear.

Student: (looks at card) *Eat...*

You: *...ate... eaten. Is that right?*

Student: (checks the card) *Yes, that's right!*

Pre-teach *Yes, that's right!* and *No, try again!* for the students to use as responses. Student B then tests Student A using his/her card. Give the learners a few moments to try to recall the past forms, then call out *Change!* Each pair passes both their cards on to the pair sitting next to them and the activity continues. Give feedback at the end of the game. Aim to keep this activity moving at a fairly fast pace; trying to produce the past forms before you call out *Change!* makes the activity fun.

For more able groups, this activity can be made more demanding by requiring that students make a sentence around the past participle, e.g.:

Student A: *Eat...*
Student B: *...ate...eaten. Is that right?*
Student A: *Yes, that's right!*
Student B: *OK... I have never eaten snake meat.*
Student A: *Great! OK, my turn...*

Conversation

Hold your book so that the students can see p. 33. *Say: Look at page 33. Look at the "Conversation."* Tell the students that Makoto is meeting his friend John in a London pub. Point to the picture on p. 32 again to remind them. Read the instructions aloud. When everyone is ready, play the cassette. Tell the students: *Work in pairs. Check your answers together. Did you write the same words?*

Say: *Now listen again.* Replay the tape, pausing after each blank. *Pint of lager* may cause some problems, so play it several times as necessary so that the students can write down what they hear. Play the tape through one more time without stopping and let the students check together again.

Elicit the answers and write them on the board. Explain *pint of lager*, *Oxford Street*, and the expression *Well, it's different!* If the class is good, remind them that in the introduction, we were told that Makoto was worried that he would miss Japanese food and that he secretly brought some cup noodles with him to eat while he was abroad!

Answers:
1   a pint of lager
2   London
3   been to Oxford Street
4   very busy
5   British food
6   different

Books closed. Model the conversation, or use the cassette to drill in chorus. After practicing, tell the students to look again at p. 33 and practice the conversation again, using the "read, look up, and speak" technique.

Over to you!

Read the instructions aloud and put the students in new pairs to practice. Write the following words on the board and tell the students to mark the number of syllables above the words, and to indicate which syllable is stressed, by drawing dots of different sizes, e.g.:

Sydney
Van**cou**ver (and practice that *v* sound again!)

Los **An**geles   Ta**ron**ga Zoo
Chinatown   **Dis**neyland
interesting   in**cred**ible
fan**tas**tic   **Can**ada
Cali**for**nia   **beau**tiful

Word stress and number of syllables are very difficult for Japanese students due to the regular nature of Japanese (e.g., *Sydney* is usually pronounced *Shi-do-ney*). Elicit the answers and model the correct pronunciation of these words. Have the students practice the three dialogs in pairs and monitor from a distance. Give general class feedback at the end of the exercise and nominate some students to perform their conversations for the rest of the group.

Optional Activities

How was your trip?

Ask the students if anyone has been overseas. If several students have, put the class in groups, one "overseas" person in each group. The group should ask as many questions as possible about the trip. The object of the game is to keep the person who traveled abroad talking as much as possible.

If no one in the class has been overseas, choose a famous city and elicit (or suggest) famous places and things to do and see in that place, e.g., Sydney: visit the Opera House; walk across the Harbour Bridge; go shopping in "The Rocks"; go to the aquarium in Darling Harbour; go swimming at Bondi Beach; see the view from the top of Sydney Tower; have a barbecue, etc.

Write the ideas on the board. Put the students in groups of three. Role-play: one student has been to the city abroad, the others are his/her friends in that city and talk to him/her about what he/she has done. Encourage the students to use as much English as possible to keep the conversation going.

Teacher talk

Lower-level groups can benefit from teacher talk in a variety of ways. It gives the class a break from having to produce English, and lets them hear the target structures in a natural way (i.e., you chatting to the class). It also helps to strengthen the relationship between the class and the teacher, as it allows you to step out of your role of teacher and enables the class to get to know more about you as a person.

If you have traveled around Japan at all, bring in maps, pamphlets, and photographs to show the class. Tell the class that you want to tell them about some of the places you have been to in their country. Elicit questions if possible (*Have you been to Hokkaido?* etc.) but don't be surprised if weaker groups are reluctant to ask you questions in front of their peers. Spend a few minutes talking about your trip in Japan, using the present perfect and past tense, and giving your opinion where possible (e.g., *I've been to Nikko. I went last year. This is a photo of me at the station. I really liked Nikko, especially the waterfall. It was so beautiful!*).

Activity

Read the instructions aloud and read through the example given at the bottom of the page. Check that the students understand and can pronounce all the adjectives listed. Tell the class that they should try to find a different person to ask each of the ten questions and note down their name only next to the question. You may need to pre-teach *bullet train* (the *shinkansen*).

Move chairs and desks to the side of the room if possible, and have the whole class play the *Find someone who…* game. You may want to join in for a few minutes initially, to get the class started. When everyone is playing, monitor from a distance and make mental notes of any problem areas.

Give feedback on any serious errors at the end of the game. Ask some general feedback questions, e.g., *Who has been scuba diving? Kenji has? Kenji, where did you go scuba diving? What did you think of it?*

Finishing the lesson

Bring the class back together and congratulate them on their hard work. Tell the students to look again at the *Background notes* for Unit 12. List the functions on the board and elicit an example for each one. Write the examples too, e.g.:

Offering someone a drink:
What would you like to drink?

Asking and expressing opinions:
What do you think of Japanese food?

Talking about experiences:
Have you been to the Gold Coast?
Yes, I have. It was great!

Ask the students to copy down the examples. Assign any review homework you feel is necessary. Tell the class that in the next lesson, they will learn how talk about their plans.

Ask the students to read the *Background notes* to Unit 13 before the next lesson.

Optional Activity

Review: past participle tic-tac-toe

(Small groups only: not more than around 14 students.)

Books closed. Divide the class into two teams. Draw a large tic-tac-toe grid on the board, five squares by five squares. Write a verb in each square like this:

make	write	lose	fly	get
try	drive	eat	have	catch
take	go	see	visit	ride
tell	drink	buy	speak	lose
forget	sleep	wear	sit	play

Allocate *X* to one team and *O* to the other. Tell the class that the object of the game is to make a line of four using *X* or *O*. They do this by asking a question, using the present perfect tense of the verb in a square of their choice. If the question is completely grammatically correct, they write an *X* or an *O* in that square. If the question is not correct, tell the class that it is wrong but not what the mistake is, as the other team may want to try that square.

Make sure that all the students on the teams take a turn at asking a question. (If you like, you can answer the question but the answers are not relevant to the game.)

This game is a simple way to review the present perfect and can be repeated as many times as you like, by writing new verbs on the board. Choosing the more difficult examples (e.g., *drive*) and putting them in the center squares makes the game more challenging.

Example game:

T: *OK, Team 1. Who is going first?*
S: *Me!*
T: *OK, Sanae. Which square do you want?*
S: *GO.*
T: *Fine. What's your question?*
S: *Have you ever been to Kyoto?*
T: *Excellent!* (Teacher draws an *X* in the square). *Yes, I have. I went last spring and it was wonderful. OK, Team 2. Who's first?*
S: *Me.*
T: *All right, Mitsue. Which square?*
S: *SEE.*
T: *What's your question?*
S. *Have you saw Mt. Fuji?*
T: *Sorry, Mitsue. There's a mistake there. Team 1, can you make a question with SEE?*

The game progresses like this. The first team to make a line of four using *X* or *O* wins the game.

Unit 13
I won't be home for lunch today

Topic / functions

Saying what your plans are

Saying what time you'll be home

Apologizing for changing your plans

Review

Socializing in a café

Put the following chain dialog on the board. Put students in pairs and give an example for the first box. Students A and B are friends; Student B is a visitor to Student A's country. (Tell the students to choose a country.) Students should not write the conversation but use the boxes as prompts to create a spoken conversation. At the end of the activity, nominate a few students and listen to their conversation.

Student A   **Student B**

Ask what Student B would like to drink.
What would you like to drink …?

Answer the question.

Ask if Student B is enjoying his/her vacation.

Answer the question. Tell Student A what you did yesterday.

Ask what it was like.

Answer the question.

Ask if Student B has tried … (a food) yet.

Answer the question.

Have the students practice several times, using different information each time.

Warming up

Preview: Background notes for Unit 13

Books closed. Remind the students about the background reading they did for Unit 13. Ask students how they find out what is happening in the town they visit, to elicit *tourist information office, newspapers, guidebooks, asking your host family or friends*, etc.

Tell the class that when they visit a foreign country, they will need to be able to talk about their plans for the day, especially if they are going to stay with a family.

Open your books

Ask the class to look at the picture on p. 34. Elicit the names of the people in the picture (Koji and Mr. Todd, the homestay "father"), and read the caption aloud: *Koji is telling Mr. Todd his plans for the day.*

Listening

Read the instructions aloud. When everyone is ready, play the tape and monitor to check that everyone understands and is completing the task. After the first time through, have the students check their answers in pairs. Replay the tape, this time pausing after each question so that students can change their answers if they like. If the group is having difficulties, replay the key parts of the conversations (e.g., *I'm meeting my friends at the swimming pool*) and pause after playing them.

Play the dialogs through one more time without stopping. Have the students check their answers together one more time. Elicit the answers by taking a class vote and write them on the board.

> *Answers:*
> 1 a swimming pool
> 2 a barbecue
> 3 a Japanese restaurant
> 4 to the zoo

Look and learn

Books closed. Drill the questions and answers. If possible, bring in pictures or draw simple stick pictures on the board, of someone going to the zoo, going out with friends, going shopping, etc., and use the pictures as prompts for a substitution drill. *I haven't decided yet* was taught in Unit 10 but remind the class of the meaning as necessary.

False beginners may be familiar with the use of *will* or *going to* to express future time. Tell the class that using the *-ing* form (students do not need, at this level, to be taught grammatical terms such as "present continuous") is a very common and easy way to talk about the future when referring to your plans.

Remind the class that it is polite to let your homestay family know if you change your plans. *I'm sorry, but…* is a polite way to let them know. Teach different ways to say approximately when referring to times, e.g., *around, about, -ish*.

After modeling and practicing all the questions and answers, have the students open their books again to p. 34 and practice in pairs.

Higher-level groups may be able to start substituting their own information into the *Look and learn* answers as well.

Conversation

Hold your book so that the students can see p. 35. Say: *Look at page 35. Look at the "Conversation."* Read the instructions aloud and point to the picture on p. 34 to remind the students about Koji talking to Mr. Todd, his homestay "father." Remind the students that Koji is going to a language school in Sydney to study English, and tell the class that most language schools abroad offer social activity programs to take students to famous places in the area.

Pre-teach *Aussie* (slang for Australian) and *I'm not sure exactly* before the students listen to the tape.

Give the class a few minutes to complete the conversation by themselves. If the class is weak, tell the students to work in pairs to fill in the blanks.

When everyone is ready, play the tape through without stopping. Tell the class to check their answers together in pairs. Play the conversation again, this time stopping after each blank, so that the students can change their answers if they wish. Play the cassette one more time without stopping.

Elicit the answers and write them on the board.

Answers:
1 b **2** e **3** c **4** d **5** a

Books closed. Model the conversation, or use the cassette, drilling in chorus. After sufficient practice, have the students open their books and practice in pairs, using the "read, look up, and speak" technique. Monitor and offer help and corrections where necessary.

Over to you!

The class should be familiar with this type of exercise by this stage. Put them in pairs and read the instructions aloud. Model the correct pronunciation of *Bondi Beach*, *Stratford-upon-Avon*, and *The Mall of America* . If you have pictures of any of these places bring them into class to show the students. (Tourist offices are a good source of colorful pamphlets and

brochures.) Have the students practice, and monitor for any pronunciation problems. At the end of the role-play, have some students perform their conversations for the rest of the group.

Inventive classes may be able to make similar conversations, referring to places in Japan.

Optional Activity

Dictation and interview activity

Dictate the following questions to the class and have them write them down in a list.

What are your plans after class?

Do you have any plans for this evening?

What are you doing this weekend?

What are you doing for lunch tomorrow?

What time will you be back home tonight?

Have the students ask you the questions to start with, to give examples and to make the meanings of the questions clear to everyone.

Tell the class to interview two or three classmates by asking the questions, but they should note down only one-word or short answers (not sentences).

Monitor from a distance to check that everyone is using the present continuous to talk about their plans. At the end of the activity, give any important feedback, and elicit some of the more interesting answers you heard as you monitored.

Activity

Bring in a map of Canada and put it on the board. Remind the students that Miki and Rie are going to visit Canada on their trip. If possible, bring in pictures of any of the places mentioned in the activity (tourist offices provide free brochures and can be a good source for pictures of famous places).

Read the instructions aloud. Put the students in new pairs and allocate roles. Remind the students to cover the *Conversation* and *Look and learn* sections to make the activity as free as possible. Model the names of the places before the students start, and pre-teach *binoculars*.

If your class enjoys acting out the activities, give each pair some background information so that they have a more detailed role to play. For example:

Host parents
While talking to your guest, you are cooking breakfast in the kitchen/washing the car/cleaning the living room/watching an interesting program on TV.

Homestay guest
While talking to your host parent, you are eating a piece of toast/late and trying to leave in a hurry/making a cup of coffee using the coffee maker.

Have some of the students perform their role-plays for the rest of the group.

Finishing the lesson

Bring the class together and congratulate them on their efforts. Tell the students to look again at the *Background notes* for Unit 13. List the functions on the board and elicit an example for each one. Write the examples too, e.g.:

Saying what your plans are:
> *I'm meeting Rie for coffee.*

Saying what time you'll be home:
> *I should be home around six o'clock.*

Apologizing for changing your plans:
> *Sorry, but I won't be home for dinner tonight.*

Ask the class to copy down the examples. Assign any review homework you feel is necessary. Tell the class that in the next lesson, they will learn how to catch the right bus.

Ask the students to read the *Background notes* to Unit 14 before the next class.

Optional Activity

Review: dialog ordering

Books closed. Write the following mixed-up dialog on the board. Ask the students to read the sentences and to write the conversation in the correct order. This makes it much easier to practice, rather than having to search for the next sentence each time they speak. Start them off by telling them which sentence starts the conversation (3).

1   Oh, I'm sorry, Mrs. Scott. I forgot to tell you. I won't be home for dinner tonight.

2   That's a good idea. And then this evening, Sarah's asked me to dinner to meet her sister.

3   Are you going out, Junko? See you at dinner, then.

4   That's fine. Well, see you tonight!

5   How nice of her! What time will you be back?

6   Well, I'm going to the Modern Art Museum this afternoon.

7   Around nine thirty, I think.

8   Oh, that's OK. You're telling me now! What are your plans today?

9   Oh, it's a very interesting museum. You should buy some postcards there.

Check that everyone has written down the conversation correctly and have them practice in pairs.

Answers:

3, 1, 8, 6, 9, 2, 5, 7, 4

Unit 14
Could you tell me when we're there, please?

Topic / functions
Asking for information about buses
Asking the price of a bus ticket
Asking for help

Review

Talking about your plans
Put these words up on the board:

plans	sorry
home	The Statue of Liberty
time	around 9:30
sightseeing	dinner
today	Bye!

Books closed. Tell students to work in pairs to make a short conversation using all the words on the board. If the group struggles, allow them to look briefly at *Look and learn* on p. 34 of their books to remind themselves of the structures to use.

You may want to replay the *Conversation* from Unit 13 one more time to the class if they had difficulties with the review activity.

Warming up

Preview: Background notes for Unit 14
Books closed. Remind the students about the background reading they did for Unit 14. Write some of the more difficult vocabulary on the board and elicit or teach definitions for them. Ask the class to make a note of any new words in their vocabulary books. For example:

a timetable: a plan of the bus times/routes (bring in an authentic timetable to show the class)
combination / special ticket: a ticket that lets you make several trips in one day and which you can sometimes use on other forms of transportation such as trams, or the subway (U.S.)/underground (U.K.)
fare: the price for a bus or train ticket
student fare: a special price for students. You will need to show your student card or identification when you buy a student ticket

bus conductor: a person who sells tickets on the bus (e.g., in London, on some buses)

Being able to understand and use bus timetables in a foreign language is a skill, and mastering it will help your students gain a great deal of independence and confidence on their trip abroad.

If you have any authentic examples from your country, bring them in for the class to look at. Point out that services often change on the weekends and public holidays, as in Japan. Using public transportation such as buses often requires more confidence than using the subways, for example, because bus stops often have no names and, unlike in Japan, stops are usually unannounced. Therefore, traveling by bus requires the courage to ask strangers for help. Tell the class that in this unit, they will learn how to ask for help.

Open your books

Tell the students to look at p. 36. Point to the picture and read the caption: *Koji is going to the beach by bus.*

Listening

Read the instructions aloud. Read through the sentences and tell the students to listen carefully to the conversations. When everyone is ready, play the cassette and monitor to check that everyone is completing the task. Tell the class: *Work together in pairs. Check your answers. Did you circle the same answers?*

Say: *Now listen again.* Replay the tape, this time pausing after each dialog. If the class is struggling, replay the key sentences (e.g., *No, the six. That's the one you need.*) and pause after playing them.

Tell the students to check again in pairs. Play the tape one more time, and elicit the answers by nominating students. Write the answers on the board.

Answers:
1 F **2** T **3** F **4** F **5** F **6** F

Look and learn

Books closed. Drill the questions and answers chorally. Tell the students that Balmain and Manly are both places in Sydney. If you don't want to distract the students with names, use place names that the students are familiar with.

Model *Could you tell me when we're there, please?* carefully. The class may struggle as the sounds *we're* and *there* are next to each other in the sentence. Place the sentence stress on *there*.

Students open their books to p. 36 and practice in pairs. If you prefer, have them substitute local names and prices as well as practicing the new place names.

Write a number of place names, bus numbers, and prices on the board, and tell the students to substitute the new information into their questions and answers, e.g.:

the city center	501
5A	£2.30
$1.75	£1.25
107	the conference center
the shopping mall	

Conversation

Hold your book so that the students can see p. 37. Say: *Look at page 37. Look at the "Conversation."* Read the instructions aloud and give the students time to complete the conversation speculatively. Stronger classes should complete the dialog individually, but allow less confident groups to work in pairs. Tell the class that *Sorry. What was that?* means the same as *Pardon me?*

Say: *Now listen. Check your answers. Did you get it right?* Play the cassette through once and have the students check together.

Say: *Now listen again.* Replay the cassette, pausing after each blank so that students have time to change their answers if they wish. If necessary, play the cassette one more time through without stopping.

Check the answers as a class. Write the conversation on the board and have different students fill in the blanks. Alternatively, nominate students to tell you the answers and write them on the board.

Answers:
1 b **2** e **3** a **4** c **5** d

Books closed. Model the conversation, or use the cassette, drilling chorally. Explain *It leaves in ten minutes*, if there is confusion. Check that the students are comfortable with reading the bus fare and remind them of different ways of saying prices (e.g., $2.50 = *two dollars and fifty cents, two fifty*). Tell the class that *er* and *um* are noises we make when hesitating (equivalent to *ano* and *eto* in Japanese).

Books open. Have the students practice the conversation in pairs, using the "read, look up and speak" technique. Monitor and give help if the students ask. Give feedback on any pronunciation and intonation problems at the end of the exercise.

Optional Activity

Bus timetables

Write the following part of a bus timetable on the board:

Oxford Bus Station	Heathrow Airport Central Bus Station (Terminals 1, 2, and 3)	Heathrow Airport Terminal 4	Gatwick South Terminal	Gatwick North Terminal
0930 →	1040 →	1100		
1030 →	1140 →	1200		
1100 →	1210 →	→	1305 →	1310
1130 →	1240 →	1300		
1230 →	1340 →	1400		
1330 →	1440 →	1500		
1400 →	1510 →	→	1605 →	1610

	Heathrow	Gatwick
Single	£9.00	£15.00
Return	£10.00	£16.00

Tell the students that they are in Oxford and are going to fly home today. Pre-teach *terminal*, *single* and *return* (U.K. English; U.S. equivalents are *one way* and *round trip*). Show the class where Heathrow and Gatwick airports are on a map of the U.K.

Tell the students to make new conversations using the information on the board, imagining what time they would like to leave and which airport and terminal they need. This exercise gives practice in reading timetables, including understanding the 24-hour-clock. If your class is not familiar with 24-hour-clock times, spend a few minutes on this area before they start. Pre-teach *It's the first/second/third/last stop*.

Nominate some pairs to act out their conversations for the rest of the group at the end of the activity.

Over to you!

Ask the students which countries these characters are visiting: Mayumi (U.K.), Miki (U.S.), Koji (Australia). Read through the instructions. Model the pronunciation of *British Museum*, *Chinatown*, and *Balmain*, and remind the class how to read prices in pounds if necessary.

Have the students practice in pairs and monitor from a distance. Students who require more practice should invent their own conversations, using local place names and prices. Have some pairs act out their conversations for the rest of the class.

Optional Activity

Using the tapescript

If your class is of quite a high level and they enjoy drama activities, make copies of the *Listening* dialogs and cut them up. Put the students in new pairs and give each pair one of the dialogs. Replay the *Listening* and ask the class to listen and read through their one dialog silently as the cassette plays. Give the class 10–15 minutes to practice acting out their conversations. Higher-level groups can adapt the tapescript if they wish. Move the desks and have the students set up the chairs to represent buses/bus stops.

Monitor the exercise and offer help if asked by the students. At the end of the practice time, ask students to perform their role-plays for the rest of the group.

Activity

New partners. Read the instructions aloud and allocate roles. Tell the class to cover the *Conversation* and *Look and learn* sections to make the activity as free as possible. Model the bus stop names before the students start practicing. Have them practice several times and ask them to change roles halfway through. Monitor unobtrusively and note any areas which need reviewing as a class. Write some of the mistakes that you heard on the board at the end of the role-play and ask the students to work in pairs to correct them. Elicit the answers and correct the mistakes on the board.

Optional Activity

Fill in the blanks

Books closed. Write the following dialog on the board and ask the students to copy it down and work in pairs to fill in the blanks. For weaker groups, write the missing words, mixed up, in a separate column on the board. (The dialog is given here with the answers in place.)

A: *Excuse me.*
B: *Yes? Can I help you?*
A: *Yes, please. Which bus goes to the city center?*
B: *I'm sorry, what was that?*
A: *Sorry, my English isn't very good yet. Is this the bus for the city center?*
B: *Oh, no, it isn't. You want the number 501.*
A: *Oh, really? What time is the next 501?*
B: *I'll just check for you. Oh, it's soon. It'll be here in about five minutes.*
A: *Oh, great! Thank you very much for your help.*
B: *No problem.*

Ask some volunteers to write the missing words in the blanks on the board. Tell the class to practice the conversation in pairs.

Finishing the lesson

Bring the class back together after the activity and congratulate them for their efforts. Remind higher-level groups that in many countries, bus stops are not announced and so when traveling by bus, it is important for them to be able to ask for help to get off the bus at the right stop.

Tell the class to look again at the *Background notes* for Unit 14. List the functions on the board and elicit an example for each one. Write the examples too, e.g.:

Asking for information about buses:
    Which bus goes to Manly?
Asking the price of a bus ticket:
    How much is it to Balmain?
Asking for help:
    Could you tell me when we're there, please?

Tell the class to copy down the examples. Assign any review homework you feel is necessary. Tell the class that in the next lesson, they will learn how to ask and answer questions in a store and how to pay for things.

Ask the class to read the *Background notes* for Unit 15 before the next class.

Optional Activity

Vocabulary review: traveling by bus

Write these scrambled words on the board and ask the students to decode them in pairs. Ask the students to ask their partner a question using each word.

1	sub	(*bus*)	e.g., *Which bus goes to the zoo?*
2	ciettk	(*ticket*)	e.g., *Where do I buy a ticket?*
3	mite	(*time*)	e.g., *What time is the next bus?*
4	meburn	(*number*)	e.g., *What number bus goes to the shopping center?*
5	tge ffo	(*get off*)	e.g., *Could you tell me when to get off, please?*

With higher-level groups, repeat the activity using other lexis, e.g., *bus terminal*, *student ticket*.

Unit 15
How would you like to pay?

Topic / functions

Talking about things in stores

Asking about prices

Asking about payment

Review

Traveling by bus: scrambled dialog

Write the following mixed-up dialog between a passenger and bus driver on the board and ask the students to work in pairs to put it in the correct order. Check their answers and ask them to practice the conversation in pairs.

1 How far are you going?
2 That's right.
3 Excuse me. Is this the bus for Northbridge Junction?
4 Are you going all the way to Northbridge?
5 Oh, I see. No, I'm not. I'm going to Bonds Corner.
6 Oh, good! How much is it, please?
7 Sure, no problem.
8 Bonds Corner? OK. That's $3.30, please.
9 How far? I'm sorry, I don't understand.
10 Here you are. Er, could you tell me when to get off, please?
11 Thank you very much!

Answers:
3, 2, 6, 1, 9, 4, 5, 8, 10, 7, 11

Warming up

Preview: Background notes for Unit 15

Books closed. Remind the students about the background reading they did for Unit 15. Write the following chart on the board:

	Japan	(your country)
Most stores open at:		
Most stores close at:		
Days stores are open:		
Days stores are closed:		
Methods of payment:		

Ask the class questions to elicit the information about stores in Japan. Encourage as much information as possible (e.g., on which public holidays stores are closed). Then have the students ask you questions and complete the other half of the chart. Draw the students' attention to similarities and differences. If you have any students who have been abroad, ask them about their "shopping experiences" abroad and when the stores were open/closed.

Brainstorm methods of payment and remind the students (from Unit 3) that you pay *by* check, *by* traveler's check, *by* credit card or *with* a credit card, and *in* cash. If you have a personal checkbook, bring it into class to show the students (personal checkbooks are not used in Japan).

Open your books

Tell the students to look at p. 38. Remind them that Makoto and Mayumi are on their honeymoon in the U.K. and that Mayumi loves shopping. Read the caption aloud: *Mayumi and Makoto are shopping in London.* Ask some general questions to higher-level classes: *What is Makoto carrying? Does he look happy? Why not? What do you think Mayumi is saying? How much do you think it costs? What is this woman's job? What is going to happen next?* etc.

Listening

Read through the instructions. Remind the class that *method of payment* means things like cash, check, etc. Check that the students understand that they must write how much things cost and how the person paid. Read the sentences aloud before playing the tape.

When everyone is ready, play the cassette and monitor to see that everyone is completing the task. If necessary, stop after the first dialog to give the students the chance to check their answers together in pairs. Play the next three dialogs. Tell the students: *Work in pairs. Check your answers together. Do you have the same answers?*

Say: *Now listen again*. Play the cassette again, this time pausing after each dialog. If the group is having difficulties, replay the key sentences (e.g., *Credit card, then. Do you accept Visa?*) and pause after playing them.

Tell the students to check again in pairs. Play the tape one more time and elicit the answers by nominating students. Write the answers on the board so that the students can check the numbers and their spelling (some learners may have written *Visa* as opposed to *credit card*: accept both as correct).

Answers:

1 a £58
   b credit card (Visa)
2 a medium
   b $55
3 a black
   b cash
4 a 8½
   b traveler's check

If your class struggled with the prices, spend a few minutes on review by writing a list of prices on the board, using a variety of currencies. Have the class ask and answer in pairs: *How much is it? It's…* for practice. Check the answers after a few minutes.

Look and learn

Books closed. Draw a stick picture of a salesclerk and a customer on the board, or be ready to act out the roles as you model the questions and answers in the *Look and learn*. If you use pictures, point to the appropriate person as you say his or her line. Use gestures to make the meanings clear (*size, something bigger, Can I try this on?* etc.). If possible, bring in a bag of clothes to use during the drill (see the note on p.00 regarding substitution drills):

T: *May I help you?*
SS: *May I help you?*
T: *Yes. I'm looking for a cotton shirt.*
SS: *Yes. I'm looking for a cotton shirt.*
T: *May I help you? Answer!*
SS: *Yes. I'm looking for a cotton shirt.*
T: *May I help you?* (holds up a red skirt) *Red skirt!*
SS: *Yes. I'm looking for a red skirt.*

Remind the class that for S, M, and L sizes we say *small, medium,* and *large*.

Books open to p. 38. Have the students practice the questions and answers in pairs.

Optional Activities

Clothes brainstorming

Put the class into small groups. Have them stand up in a circle, and take turns saying an item of clothing, e.g., S1 *hat* S2 *skirt* S3 *shirt* S4 *jacket* S1 *shoes*.

If any student cannot think of a new word, or if they repeat an item, they must sit down. The last person left standing is the winner.

Monitor this game carefully. There are a number of words in Japanese English related to clothing that you will need to teach your class not to use. Teach their English equivalents and ask the class to remember to use them, e.g., *sweatshirt* instead of *trainer*, *striped shirt* instead of *border shirt*, *T-shirt* instead of *T-shirts*.

Class fashion show: clothes and adjectives practice

This activity is best used with stronger classes, and is not suitable for inhibited groups who do not enjoy drama activities.

Spend a few minutes teaching the adjective order we use when talking about nouns:

How big? → How old? → What color? → Where from? → Made of? → Noun

e.g., *a large blue shirt, a black leather jacket, a new Italian evening gown.*

Elicit or pre-teach as many materials as possible (e.g., *cotton, denim, leather, suede, polyester,* etc.). Tell the class to write one or two sentences about the clothes that they are wearing. Write this model on the board, substituting information about yourself:

Here's (Sophie). She's wearing (a white cotton blouse, a new gold necklace, baggy blue denim jeans, and black leather boots).

Monitor the writing stage and offer help as necessary. When everyone is ready, ask the class to swap papers with the person sitting next to them. Play some funky fashion show music in the background, and have the students take turns walking across the room, in front of the class, as their partners read the commentary they have written. If you can arrange it, having a couple of your colleagues come in to model while you commentate adds a touch of hilarity to the fashion show.

Give feedback at the end.

Conversation

Hold your Student's book so that the students can see p. 39. Say: *Look at page 39. Look at the "Conversation."* Read the instructions aloud and point to the picture on p. 38 again to remind the students about Mayumi shopping in London.

Play the cassette through once and have the students check together in pairs. Replay the conversation, pausing after each blank to give the students time to check their answers and change any information they couldn't catch the first time. If your group is struggling, replay the information to go in the blanks several times.

Let the class check their answers again in pairs. Elicit the answers and write them on the board.

Answers:

1 blouse
2 Small
3 something in white
4 This one's £85.
5 take it
6 Do you take American Express?

Books closed. Model the conversation, or use the cassette, to drill in chorus. Explain *Would you like to come this way?* After sufficient practice, have the students open their books to p. 39 and practice the *Conversation* in pairs, using the "read, look up, and speak" technique.

Over to you!

Pre-teach *moccasins* and the expression *something more colorful*. Read the instructions. Have the class practice in pairs and monitor from a distance. Listen especially for any problems with the prices and give feedback on any problem areas at the end of the exercise. Have some pairs act out their conversations for the rest of the class.

Activity

New partners. Read the instructions aloud and allocate roles. Tell the class to cover the *Conversation* and *Look and learn* sections to make the activity as free as possible. If your students will be traveling to the U.K. or Australia, pre-teach *trousers* or *slacks* instead of *pants*.

Encourage the students to practice several times and to pay in different ways. If you have toy money, hand it out before the students start. Ask the class to change roles halfway through. Monitor and give feedback on any errors at the end of the exercise. (Listen especially for any errors related to plurals, e.g., *How much are these pants?*) Ask some pairs to perform their role-play for the rest of the class.

Optional Activity

Shopping: class role-play

Take in as much "store" realia as possible (toy money and credit cards, coat hangers, sticky labels to write prices on, long mirrors, etc.). Either take in a mixed bag of clothes or ask the students to donate items for the role-play. Hang the items around the room and put prices on them. Allocate about a quarter of the class to play salesclerks. Tell the rest of the class to go shopping and use only English. You may wish to play a part yourself for a few minutes to get the activity started. Monitor the activity and give feedback at the end.

Finishing the lesson

Bring the class back together and tell the class to return to their places. Congratulate the class on their efforts. Tell them to look again at the *Background notes* for Unit 15. List the functions on the board and elicit an example for each one. Write the examples too, e.g.:

Talking about things in stores:
  I'm looking for a shirt.

Asking about prices:
  How much are these?

Asking about payment:
  Do you take American Express?

Tell the class to copy down the examples. Assign any review homework you feel is necessary. If you are planning to go straight on to Unit 16 next time, tell the class that they will learn how to send things at the post office. Ask the class to read the *Background notes* for Unit 16 before the next lesson. If you are going to spend a whole lesson on the *Out and About 3*, leave the *Background notes* reading until next time.

Optional Activity

Review: clothes vocabulary

Put the students in small groups. Make one copy of photocopiable page O (p. 94) for each group and cut up the pages into cards. Write on the board: *If I went ..., I'd wear ...*

Tell the students to take turns in their groups to pick a card and to read the sentence on the board aloud, substituting the information on the card and using their imagination to complete the sentence. Do an example first to demonstrate, rather than explain, the activity, e.g., pick the card which reads *on a picnic*, and say: *If I went on a picnic, I'd wear a long white pretty dress, a large yellow sunhat, and an old pair of sandals.*

Students take turns in their groups to pick a card and make a sentence. At the end of the activity, ask some questions to some of the groups for feedback. Give general feedback on any serious errors you heard.

Out and About 3
Getting around

Read through the notes in the introduction on p. 7 first, for additional ideas on how to use the *Out and About* pages.

This unit teaches some of the additional language that students might need to use as they travel around the country they are visiting. As a warm-up, brainstorm different forms of transportation in groups, and pre-teach *tram* if the class doesn't know it.

Remind the class that, unlike in Japan, taxi doors don't shut automatically and they should close the door themselves.

If your class has many car drivers in it, you may wish to teach them useful phrases for driving abroad (e.g., *international driver's license, car rental office, insurance, speed limit*). Remind drivers that in both Australia and the U.K. you drive on the left, as in Japan.

Ask the students to look at the pictures on pp. 40–41 of their books. Ask: *How are they traveling?*

Rie:	train (U.S.)
Koji:	tram (Australia)
Mayumi and Makoto:	London taxi (U.K.)
Koji:	motorbike (the Honda Fireblade which his Australian friend, Pete, has let him ride)
Miki:	Greyhound bus (U.S.)
Mayumi and Makoto:	London bus (U.K.)

Have the students read the conversations. Explain any vocabulary difficulties, e.g.:

Here you are	Students should know this expression by now. Teach *There you go* to higher-level classes and explain that the two expressions are interchangeable. They are both used when giving something to someone.
Is this seat free?	means *Can I sit here?* Koji is polite, because he asks before sitting in the vacant seat.
Oy!	this is much ruder in Japanese; students should not be shocked, as the cab driver is simply trying to get Makoto's attention, since he left the taxi door open. *Hey!* is another commonly used shout to get attention.

I.D.:	identification. Miki wants to buy a student ticket and so must show her student card to the clerk. Remind the students that when they change their traveler's checks, they will need some I.D. (such as their passport or driver's license).
destination	the place something/someone is going to, e.g., Makoto's destination is Hyde Park.

Model the dialogs and drill them as necessary. Have the students practice in pairs. Encourage them to memorize the expressions that they consider the most useful and to record them in their vocabulary books.

Unit 14 teaches much of the language needed when traveling by bus. However, you may want to use this unit as a springboard into further role-plays and practice activities regarding other forms of transportation. If your class consists of older learners, such as businesspeople, who may be more likely to use taxis some of the time in the foreign country, spend some time teaching "taxi" language (e.g., *Please take me to… / Can I put my bags in the back? / Could you stop here, please?*).

Train and subway routes are usually relatively easy for tourists to understand, but remind your class that stops may not be announced as frequently as they are in Japan. If your entire class is going to a particular city or area, try to obtain some *subway* (U.K.: *underground*) maps for the class to look at beforehand, and spend some time on pronunciation of the key stops.

Write five or six more "getting around" situations on the board, e.g., catching a taxi to your hotel, asking which platform your train leaves from, buying a season ticket for the bus, renting a bicycle for the day, checking what time your train leaves, asking where the dining car is on the train.

Put the students into small groups and tell them to write and practice mini-dialogs for one or two of the situations. Monitor and offer help as necessary. Have some groups act out their role-plays for the rest of the class at the end of the activity. Give feedback at the end.

Unit 16
Can I send this airmail?

Topic / functions

Making requests

Asking about mailing things

Asking about other services

Review

Shopping for clothes: matching the sentences

Books closed. Write the following on the board and ask the students to work in pairs to match each question with the correct reply. After checking the answers, have the students practice in pairs.

The questions:

1 May I help you?
2 What size are you looking for?
3 How much are these shoes?
4 Do you accept credit cards?
5 Can I try this on?
6 Do you have anything in blue?
7 How would you like to pay?

The answers:

a By traveler's check, please.
b Certainly. The fitting room is just over there.
c Yes, we do. Do you have any I.D.?
d I think I'm a size 9.
e They're $156, sir.
f No, thanks. I'm just looking.
g How about this one?

Answers:
1 f 2 d 3 e 4 c 5 b 6 g 7 a

Warming up

Preview: Background notes for Unit 16

Books closed. Remind the class about the *Background notes* they read for Unit 16. Put the following chart on the board and ask the students to work in small groups to list as many words as they can think of.

At a post office:

Things to send	Things to buy	Ways to send things

If possible, bring in as much realia (aerograms, airmail stickers, customs labels, etc.) as you can to help with the pre-teaching of useful post office vocabulary. Although it is possible to buy aerograms in Japan, many of your students may not be familiar with them and since they are so convenient to use when traveling abroad, pre-teach as necessary. List any new lexis on the board and ask students to write it down in their vocabulary books.

Open your books

Tell the students to look at p. 42. Tell the students that Mayumi is in a typical British post office. Ask the class some general questions about the picture: *What is she holding? Who is she talking to?* Read the caption aloud: *Mayumi is buying stamps at a post office.*

Listening

Read the instructions aloud. Read through the sentences and pre-teach any unknown vocabulary, e.g., *registered letter*.

When everyone is ready, play the cassette and monitor to check that everyone is completing the task. Tell the students: *Work in pairs. Check your answers together. Do you have the same answers?*

Say: *Now listen again.* Play the cassette again, this time pausing after each question to give the students time to change their answers if they wish. If the class is struggling, replay the key sentences (e.g., *I'd like to send this package, please.*) and pause after each one.

Tell the students to check again in pairs. Play the tape one more time and elicit the answers by taking a class vote. If the entire class gets an answer wrong, replay the relevant part, pause the tape, and repeat the sentence slowly yourself. Write the answers on the board.

Answers:
1 send a package
2 buy aerograms
3 buy a phonecard
4 send postcards to Europe
5 pick up a registered letter

Look and learn

Books closed. Model the questions and answers clearly. Explain *weigh*, and any other vocabulary which you didn't cover in the warming-up stage. Drill the questions and answers.

After sufficient practice, have the students open their books to p. 42 and practice asking and answering in pairs. Monitor carefully for pronunciation mistakes caused by reading the words (especially *weigh* and *registered*). Correct as necessary. Encourage the students to practice several times each.

Higher-level classes should close their books after practicing and use prompts written on the board to make their own questions and answers, e.g., *letter, postcards, stamps, package, cheapest, fastest, safest.*

Conversation

Hold your book so that the students can see p. 43. Say: *Look at page 43. Look at the "Conversation."* Read the instructions aloud and point to the picture on p. 42 again to remind the students about Mayumi in the post office. Play the cassette through once and have the students check together in pairs. Replay the conversation, pausing after each blank to give the students time to check their answers and change any information they couldn't catch the first time. If the class is having difficulties, replay the key parts and pause after each one. Have the students check in pairs once more.

Replay the conversation for the last time and elicit the answers. Check that there were no difficulties with *twelve* (often confused with *twenty*), the price in pounds, and the spelling (and meaning) of *surface*. Write the answers on the board.

> *Answers*:
> **1** twelve
> **2** Japan
> **3** £4.20
> **4** cheapest
> **5** surface mail
> **6** twelve weeks

Books closed. Model the conversation, or use the cassette, drilling in chorus. After sufficient practice, have the students open their books to p. 43 and practice in pairs. Remind them to use the "read, look up, and speak" technique.

Over to you!

Remind the class of the meanings of *express mail, registered mail,* and *surface mail* before they start. Have the class practice the new conversations together, and give feedback at the end. Have some pairs act out their conversations for the rest of the class.

Optional Activity

Writing a postcard

Higher-level classes only. If possible, bring in a few real postcards that you have received from various countries. Show the students where to write the address, date, name, and your signature. Draw a large

mock postcard on the board. Ask the class questions to elicit information and write it on the postcard, e.g.:

Ask: *Where are you on vacation?*
Here I am in New York!

Ask: *What's the weather like?*
The weather is fantastic. It's warm and sunny every day.

Ask: *What have you done?*
Yesterday I went sightseeing. I saw the Statue of Liberty and I've taken a lot of photos.

Ask: *When are you coming home?*
I'll see you when I return next week!

Best wishes,

Junko

Put the students in small groups and hand out either postcards or sheets of paper for the class to write on. Tell the groups to write a postcard to a friend in the room. Monitor and offer as much help as necessary. If your class is weak, give prompts by writing adjectives and useful phrases on the board. Put up maps and pictures of famous places to visit if you have them. At the end of the writing phase, have the students swap postcards to read.

Activity

New partners. Read the instructions aloud and allocate roles. Tell the B students to cover the *Look and learn* and *Conversation* sections, and to use the chart for information. The A students should read their role-play information and then close their books for the duration of the activity.

Spend a few minutes going over the chart before they start. Ask some general questions, e.g., *How much does it cost to send a postcard to Australia? How long does it take by surface mail?*, so that the class can understand how to use the information given. Higher-level groups should be encouraged to use as much English as they can during the role-play. Pre-teach interested students additional vocabulary such as *commemorative stamps, insurance items, customs slip, fragile, breakable,* etc.

Encourage the students to practice several times and to change roles halfway through. Monitor and give feedback on any important errors at the end. Ask some pairs to act out their role-play for the rest of the class.

Finishing the lesson

Bring the class back together and tell the students to return to their places. Congratulate the class on their efforts. Tell them to look at the *Background notes* for Unit 16. List the functions on the board and elicit an example for each one. Write the examples too, e.g.:

Making requests:
Could I have five stamps for Japan, please?

Asking about mailing things:
What's the safest way to send this to Japan?

Asking about other services:
Do you sell phonecards here?

Tell the class to copy down the examples. Assign any review homework you feel is necessary. Tell the class that in the next lesson, they will learn about going to the theater. If any of your students have seen any famous musicals or similar, ask them to bring their souvenir programs to show the class next time.

Ask the students to read the *Background notes* for Unit 17 before the next class.

Optional Activity

Review: post office vocabulary

Books closed. Write the following words with missing letters on the board and tell the students that they used these in Unit 16. Can they guess what the words are? The first student to finish is the winner!

1 _ o s _   o _ _ i c e
2 l e _ _ e r
3 s _ a _ p
4 _ h _ _ _ c _ r d
5 p _ c _ a _ e
6 p o s _ _ _ _ d
7 c h _ _ p _ s t
8 f a _ _ e s _

Answers:

1 post office
2 letter
3 stamp
4 phonecard
5 package
6 postcard
7 cheapest
8 fastest

Unit 17
What time does the show start?

Topic / functions
Asking about tickets
Asking about times
Asking about location

Review

In a post office: choose the best response

Books closed. Write the following questions and answers on the board. Have the students copy them down and put a check by the best responses. After checking their answers, have the students practice in pairs.

1 I'd like to send this airmail to Japan.
  a About six days.
  b Yes, we do.
  c I'll need to weigh it.
2 What's the fastest way to send this?
  a By express mail.
  b By surface mail.
  c By registered mail.
3 Do you sell phonecards here?
  a Sure. Where to?
  b Yes, we do.
  c By airmail.
4 Could I have seven stamps for these postcards, please?
  a It's safest by registered mail.
  b I'm afraid we don't, sir.
  c Certainly. Where to?
5 How much does it cost to send a letter to Japan?
  a It's too expensive.
  b It depends on the weight.
  c It takes about one week.

Answers:
1c 2a 3b 4c 5b

Warming up

Preview: Background notes for Unit 17

Books closed. Remind the class about the *Background notes* they read for Unit 17. Ask if any of your students have ever seen a musical or a show, where they saw it, and how much it cost. If you have any programs or posters from any productions, bring them in to show the class. See if the students can tell you some of the different ways of buying tickets mentioned in the *Background notes*. Remind the class that Miki is in New York.

Open your books

Tell the class to look at p. 44. Point to the picture and ask some general questions about it: *Where are Miki and Rie? Which show do you think they want to see? What is going to happen next?* etc. Read the caption aloud: *Miki and Rie are buying tickets for a show.*

Listening

Read the instructions aloud. Read through the sentences and tell the students that *dress circle* and *front stalls* are different seating places in the *theater* (U.K. spelling: *theatre*). They will look at this more carefully in the language study section. Remind the class of the meaning of *true* and *false* if there are any problems.

When everyone is ready, play the cassette and monitor to check that everyone is completing the task. Say: *Work in pairs. Check your answers together. Do you have the same answers?*

Say: *Now listen again.* Replay the tape, if necessary, pausing after the key sentences (e.g., *...that's too expensive ...Thanks anyway.*).

Tell the students to check in pairs again. Play the tape one more time and elicit the answers by taking a class vote. If everyone gets the wrong answer to a question, replay the relevant part, pause the tape, and repeat the part yourself. Write the answers on the board.

Answers:
1 F 2 T 3 F 4 T

With higher-level groups, you may wish to spend a few minutes going over the listening exercises more thoroughly, replaying parts of the cassette and possibly using the tapescript. Useful phrases to look at here would include *Thanks anyway / Someone is sitting in my seat / The stairs are over there / I loved it!*

Look and learn

Books closed. Draw a stick picture on the board of a ticket clerk and a customer at a ticket booth. Draw a thought bubble coming from the customer's head and elicit things that he/she needs to ask. Write these in the bubble, e.g., *tonight, time, how much?* Drill the questions and answers, pointing to the picture to indicate which person is speaking. Explain *obstructed view* by drawing on the board or acting out. If your students will be visiting a particular country, try to bring in a real *subway* (U.K. *underground*) map, and a map of where some of the famous theaters are.

Have the students open their books to look at the diagrams showing different parts of the theater and their names.

Have the students practice the questions and answers in pairs.

Optional Activity

Asking about movies

Although most visitors abroad on short visits will want to go to see a musical or show, those who stay for longer periods (e.g., Koji on his Working Holiday Visa) are quite likely to *go to the movies* as well (U.K. *go to the cinema / to see a film*).

Some of the questions in the language study can be practiced as telephone questions to the movie theater, asking about movies that are showing that night. Have a class brainstorm about different kinds of movie (comedy, action, mystery, horror, love story, etc.) and write four or five on the board. Elicit one movie title for each category and write it, with a time and price underneath. Tell the students to practice in pairs, calling the theater and asking questions to find out about starting times, ticket prices, etc. Pre-teach some useful questions and do an example first with a good student, e.g.:

S: *Hello, ABC cinema.*

T: *Hello. What's showing tonight?*

S: *E.T.*

T: *Oh, I love that movie! What time does it start, please?*

S: *Two o'clock, five o'clock, and eight-thirty.*

T: *What time does the eight-thirty show finish?*

S: *At ten forty-five.*

T: *OK. How much are the tickets?*

S: *$6.00 for adults, $3.00 for students and children under twelve.*

T: *That's fine. Thanks for your help. Bye.*

S: *Goodbye.*

Have the students practice making their own conversations in pairs.

Conversation

Hold your Student's book so that the students can see p. 45. Say: *Look at page 45. Look at the "Conversation."* Read the instructions aloud and point to the picture on p. 44 again to remind the class about Miki and Rie buying tickets. Give the class time to complete the conversation speculatively before listening to the tape.

Pre-teach *rear* and *matinée*.

Play the tape and let the students check their answers in pairs. Replay the tape, pausing after each blank to give the class time to change their answers if they wish.

Play the conversation through one more time without stopping. Elicit the answers and write them on the board.

Answers:
1 c 2 f 3 d 4 b 5 e 6 a

Books closed. Model the conversation, or use the cassette, drilling chorally. After sufficient practice, have the students open their books to p. 45 again and practice the conversation in pairs.

Over to you!

New pairs. Read the instructions and have the students practice the new dialogs. Model the pronunciation of *Figaro*, *The Mousetrap*, and *Crazy for You*, and monitor to check that there are no problems with the prices and pronunciation of the theater terms. Re-drill if necessary and give general feedback at the end. Ask some students to perform their role-plays for the rest of the group.

Optional Activities

Booking a theater ticket: split dialog

Students work in pairs. Make one copy of photocopiable page P (p. 95) for each pair of students in the class and cut the pages in half. Hand them out to Students A and B. Tell the students not to look at their partner's paper. Have the pairs sit back-to-back to simulate a telephone call to a ticket agency.

Tell Student A that he/she works in a ticket booth. Tell Student B that he/she is visiting London and wants to see a popular West End show before going home. If necessary, demonstrate the first few lines of the conversation with a student.

Monitor from a distance and give help if the students are really struggling. Weaker groups can write their lines on their page as they go along to help them when they practice through again later. Give the class enough time to understand the activity and practice it. Listen to a couple of pairs perform their conversations for the rest of the class.

Inquiring about movies

If you tried the *Optional Activity: Realia drill* on p.13 and your students found it motivating, bring in some realia in English referring to movies that are playing in Japan. English-language newspapers and magazines often have movie guides with maps and starting times indicated. Make copies of the pages and tell the students to choose a movie they'd like to see and to take turns asking and answering questions about the movie information.

Although this is a very unrealistic practice phase, as the students can see all the information, it does, however, provide useful practice reading through English guides and identifying important details.

Activity

New partners. Read the instructions aloud and allocate roles. Tell the class to cover the *Conversation* and *Look and learn* sections and to use as much English as possible. Monitor and give feedback at the end. Write some of the more important errors heard on the board and ask the students to correct them.

Ask some pairs to act out their role-play for the rest of the class.

Finishing the lesson

Bring the class back together and congratulate them on their efforts. Tell the students to look again at the *Background notes* for Unit 17. List the functions on the board and elicit an example for each one. Write the examples too, e.g.:

Asking about tickets:
  Do you have any seats for the orchestra?
Asking about times:
  What time does the show start?
Asking about location:
  What is the nearest subway station, please?

Ask the class to copy down the examples. Assign any review homework you feel is necessary. Tell the class that in the next lesson they will learn what to do if they lose something while traveling overseas.

Ask the class to read the *Background notes* for Unit 18 before the next class.

Optional Activity

Review: scrambled sentences
Write these scrambled sentences on the board and ask the students to work in pairs to reorder them correctly.

1 much the are How tickets?
2 time does finish What show the?
3 we're Sorry out sold
4 them take I'll
5 Do stalls have in seats any you the?

Answers:
1 How much are the tickets?
2 What time does the show finish?
3 Sorry, we're sold out.
4 I'll take them.
5 Do you have any seats in the stalls?

Unit 18
Where did you lose it?

Topic / functions

Reporting what you have lost, and where

Describing lost items

Talking about place and time

Review

Buying a theater ticket

Put the following chain dialog on the board. Put students in pairs and give an example for the first box. Student A is the tourist and Student B the theater ticket clerk. Students shouldn't write the conversation but use the boxes to create a spoken conversation. At the end of the activity, nominate a few students and listen to their conversations.

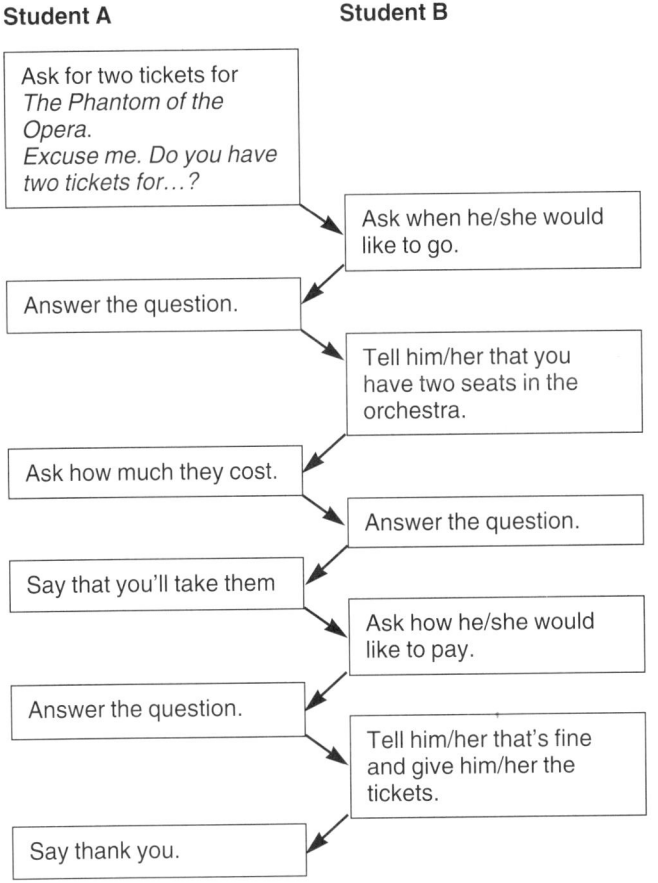

Student A | Student B

Ask for two tickets for *The Phantom of the Opera.*
Excuse me. Do you have two tickets for…?

Ask when he/she would like to go.

Answer the question.

Tell him/her that you have two seats in the orchestra.

Ask how much they cost.

Answer the question.

Say that you'll take them

Ask how he/she would like to pay.

Answer the question.

Tell him/her that's fine and give him/her the tickets.

Say thank you.

Have the students practice in pairs several times, using different information each time.

Warming up

Preview: Background notes for Unit 18

Books closed. Remind the students about the background reading they did for Unit 18. With higher-level groups, open a class discussion on ways to travel safely while abroad (e.g., not to carry large amounts of cash, to use traveler's checks, not to wear expensive jewelry, to leave valuables such as passport and airline tickets in the hotel safe).

With weaker groups, spend a few minutes brainstorming ways to describe things. Do a stick drawing on the board of a tourist talking to a hotel receptionist about a bag he has lost. The tourist should have a thought bubble with a backpack inside. Draw an empty speech bubble for the receptionist. Elicit one-word questions from the class that the receptionist might ask, and write them in the speech bubble (*where? what? how big? color? inside? expensive?* etc.).

Tell the class that in this lesson, they will learn what to do if they lose something.

Open your books

Tell the students to look at the picture on p. 46. Read the unit title aloud. Remind the class that Mayumi and Makoto are staying at a hotel in Oxford. Read the caption aloud: *Makoto has lost something.* Ask the students to guess what he might have lost.

Listening

Read through the instructions and the sentences. Explain *leather*. When everyone is ready, play the cassette and monitor to check that everyone is completing the task. Tell the students: *Work in pairs. Check your answers together. Do you have the same answers?*

Say: *Now listen again.* Replay the cassette, pausing after each dialog. If the class is having difficulties, replay the key sentences (e.g., *Oh no. It's quite small.*) and pause after each one. More able classes can also be told to write down the place where each item was lost and if it has been found.

Tell the students to check again together and play the tape through one last time without stopping. Elicit the answers and write them on the board.

Answers:
1   a small blue leather bag
2   a blue and white umbrella
3   a shopping bag with a camera in it
4   a credit card

Look and learn

Books closed. Use realia (a bag, a camera, and a purse) as props while drilling the first language box. If you have the stick drawing on the board from the listening exercise, use it again here while drilling. Erase the questions in the receptionist's speech bubble and write in *wh- ?* to show that the receptionist asks a number of *wh-* questions (*where, when, what, how*). Drill the questions and answers.

For extra practice in this controlled-practice phase, bring in several different types of bag and have the students ask you the questions about them. Have more able groups brainstorm as many different types of bag as they can think of for vocabulary practice (e.g., *backpack, briefcase, plastic bag, shoulder bag, sports bag*).

Books open. Have the class practice the questions and answers in pairs. After practicing the target structures, ask the students to practice the questions again but this time to describe their own bags in the answers. This can be much more difficult than it sounds, so be on hand to provide vocabulary and help as necessary.

Optional Activity

Describing your bag

Make enough copies of photocopiable pages Q and R (pp. 96-97) so that each pair of students can have one card. Cut up the pages and give one picture to each pair.

Demonstrate with a student how to play the game. Students sit in pairs in a circle. Student A asks *What did you lose?* Student B looks at the picture and describes the lost bag and contents. Student A can prompt by asking extra *wh-* questions. When you call out *Change!*, students pass their picture to the next pair, and then change roles so that Student B asks the questions and Student A describes the lost item.

Repeat the process until the pairs have tried most or all of the pictures. Give feedback on useful vocabulary that emerged during the exercise.

Conversation

Hold your book so that the students can see p. 47. Say: *Look at page 47. Look at the "Conversation."* Read the instructions aloud and point to the picture on p. 46 again to remind the class of Makoto. Give the class time to complete the conversation speculatively before listening to the tape. Pre-teach *missing* and *details*.

Play the cassette and let the students check their answers in pairs. Replay the cassette, pausing after each blank to give the class time to change their answers if they wish.

Play the conversation through one more time without stopping. Elicit the answers and write them on the board.

Answers:
1 e **2** c **3** a **4** d **5** b

Books closed. Model the conversation, or use the cassette, drilling in chorus. After sufficient practice, have the students open their books to p. 47 again and practice the conversation in pairs, using the "read, look up, and speak" technique.

Over to you!

New pairs. Read the instructions aloud and have the students practice the new dialogs. Monitor and give feedback on any pronunciation problems at the end of the exercise. Confident classes should act out the conversations as realistically as possible. (Teach the appropriate intonation patterns to indicate worry!)

Activity

New partners. Read the instructions aloud and allocate roles. Spend a few minutes going over the information given in the columns on p. 47 before students start.

Stretch more able classes by encouraging them to use as much English as possible during the activity. Pre-teach useful phrases that they might be able to include (e.g., *Was it insured? Were there any valuables inside?*).

Monitor from a distance and make mental notes on any problem areas. Give feedback at the end of activity.

Ask some pairs to perform their role-play for the rest of the class.

Optional Activities

Lost and Found: class role-play

Divide the class into "Lost and Found" clerks (about one third of the class) and tourists. Set up a Lost and Found table at the side of the classroom and tell the tourists to put one thing of theirs on the table (e.g., bags, umbrellas, items of clothing, watches, jewelry). The clerks should not look as the tourists do this.

Set up tables for the clerks to work from. Tell the tourists to come to the Lost and Found Office and tell the clerks what they have lost. The clerks should ask as many questions as possible (you may need to put some prompts on the board for weaker groups) before going over to the Lost and Found table to look for the item. By the end of the activity, all students should have their own things back if they have successfully described what they lost. You may want to take the part of one of the clerks for a few minutes at the beginning of the role-play to start things off. Once everyone is participating, retreat to monitor the activity.

Give feedback on any important errors you heard when the role-play is finished.

Lost and Found: contradicting people

New partners. Demonstrate the activity with a student first. Ask what they have lost and deliberately mishear one word. Have the student repeat themselves, using the appropriate word stress to indicate the mistake. Continue the conversation, asking other *wh-* questions but misunderstanding one thing each time. For example:

> T: *Can I help you?*
>
> S: *Yes, please. I've lost my suitcase.*
>
> T: *I see. Your briefcase, you said? What color is it?*
>
> S: *No, not my briefcase, my suitcase. It's red with a silver handle.*
>
> T: *Oh, your suitcase. Blue with a silver handle.*
>
> S: *Uh, no, actually it's red with a silver handle.*
>
> T: *Ah, red. Of course. When did you lose it?*
>
> S: *Tuesday morning. I left it on the train.*
>
> T: *Thursday morning? OK. What time was that?*
>
> S: *No, not Thursday, Tuesday. Tuesday morning. The ten-thirty train.*

Students play the game in their pairs, with the clerk pretending to be hard of hearing. The clerk tries to keep the conversation going as long as possible. Don't let this activity continue indefinitely: a few minutes is enough before the game becomes tiresome. Have the students change roles if the tourist becomes too frustrated!

Finishing the lesson

Bring the class back together and congratulate them on their efforts. Tell the students to look again at the Background notes for Unit 18. List the functions on the board and elicit an example for each one. Write the examples too, e.g.:

Reporting what you have lost, and where:
  I think I left a bag on the train.

Describing lost items:
  It's dark blue and made of leather.

Talking about place and time:
  On the ten o'clock bus to Oxford.

Ask the class to copy down the examples. Assign any review homework you feel is necessary. Tell the class that in the next lesson they will learn how to say goodbye to their new friends and host families before returning to Japan.

Ask the class to read the *Background notes* for Unit 19 before the next class.

Optional Activity

Review: at the Lost and Found

Books closed. Write the following on the board and ask the students to work in pairs to match each question with the reply. After checking answers, have the students practice in pairs.

The questions:

1 Where did you lose it?
2 How big is it?
3 What color is it?
4 What's it made of?
5 Was there anything inside it?

The answers:

a It's suede.
b It's quite small.
c I left it in the restaurant, under my table, I think.
d Yes, my wallet and a diary.
e It's black with a gold clasp.

Answers: **1** c **2** b **3** e **4** a **5** d

Unit 19
Goodbye and thanks!

Topic / functions

Saying goodbye

Expressing your thanks

Giving and receiving gifts

Expressing wishes for the future

Review

I've lost my bag!

Put these words on the board:

help	dark blue
bag	size
when	passport
where	address
made of	phone number

Books closed. Tell the students to work in pairs to make a short conversation using all the words on the board. If the group struggles, allow them to look back at the *Look and learn* section on p. 46. You may also wish to replay the *Conversation* from Unit 18 for weaker groups to remind them of some of the target questions they could ask and answer. Listen out for any difficulties and review any major problem areas at the end of the exercise.

Warming up

Preview: Background notes for Unit 19

Books closed. Remind the students about the Background notes they read for Unit 19. Put the class into small groups and tell them to imagine that they have been staying with a homestay family for three weeks in a foreign country. Ask them to make a list of things that they could give their family as goodbye presents.

After a few minutes, get feedback from the class and list some of their ideas on the board. Higher-level classes may be able to express good and bad points about the ideas (e.g., a *kimono* would be nice but is far too expensive unless you buy a second-hand one; paper lanterns make good presents because they are very light and easy to carry in your luggage; *sake* (rice wine) is a good present, but only if the family drinks alcohol).

Optional Activity

Saying goodbye

Elicit various ways of saying goodbye, and write them on the board. Tell the class which ones are very casual (e.g., *So long*) and which ones can be used in most situations (e.g., *Goodbye*). See if the class knows how to respond to these "goodbyes" and write some possible responses on the board. Have the students write down any unfamiliar phrases. For example:

See you tomorrow / later / tonight / next week / soon.
Yeah, see you!

So long!
Bye!

Have a nice day.
Yes, you too! Goodbye.

Goodbye. I'll miss you.
I'll miss you too.

See you on Monday.
OK. Have a good weekend!

Goodbye. It was nice meeting you.
Yes, nice meeting you too.

Open your books

Tell the students to look at p. 48. Point to the picture and remind the students that Koji has been staying with a homestay family in Sydney. Read the caption aloud: *Koji is saying goodbye to Mr. and Mrs. Todd.*

Listening

Read the instructions aloud. Explain *painting* before the students listen. When everyone is ready, play the cassette and monitor to check that everyone is completing the task. Tell the students: *Work in pairs. Check your answers together. Do you have the same answers?*

Say: *Now listen again.* Replay the cassette, if necessary, pausing after the key sentences (e.g., *Rie and I are leaving the States tomorrow.*).

Tell the students to check in pairs again. Play the tape one more time and elicit the answers by taking a class vote. Write the answers on the board.

Answers:
1 T **2** F **3** F **4** T **5** T

Look and learn

Books closed. Drill the different ways of saying *goodbye*. Explain that we use *Please say goodbye to … for me* when we won't see that person again. *This is for you* is used when giving something. Teach higher-level groups the pattern *Thank you for …-ing* and elicit other examples, e.g.: *Thank you for helping me with my English / cooking such delicious meals / being so kind / taking me to the museum / looking after me.*

Model the intonation patterns carefully for these phrases so that the students sound sincere when they give thanks for things.

Have the students open their books again to p. 48 and practice the questions and answers in pairs.

Conversation

Hold your book so that the students can see p. 49. Say: *Look at page 49. Look at the "Conversation."* Read the instructions aloud and point again to the picture on p. 48 of Koji saying goodbye to the Todds, to remind the class of the situation. Give the students time to complete the conversation speculatively before listening. Pre-teach *homesick* and *paper lantern.*

Play the tape and let the students check their answers in pairs. Replay the tape, pausing after each blank to give the class time to change their answers if they wish.

Play the conversation through one more time without stopping. Elicit the answers and write them on the board.

Answers:
1 a   **2** c   **3** d   **4** e   **5** b

Books closed. Model the conversation, or use the cassette, drilling chorally. After sufficient practice, have the students open their books again to p. 49 and practice the conversation in pairs, using the "read, look up, and speak" technique.

Over to you!

New pairs. Read the instructions and have the students practice the new dialogs. Monitor to check that there are few problems with pronunciation and intonation. Confident groups should stand up and act out the new conversations. Remind the class about their body language. Keeping eye contact, smiling, and shaking hands are all appropriate in these situations. Warn students that some host families may hug or kiss their guests, too! Learners who are having problems with their intonation could be told that a low pitch can sound very sincere.

Re-drill any problem areas and give feedback at the end of the practice phase. Ask some students to perform their conversations for the rest of the group.

Optional Activities

Thank-you cards

Draw a blank page on the board and tell the class that it's a thank-you card. Tell the class that they have been staying with a host family for two weeks in New Zealand and they will give the family this card when they leave.

Hand out blank pieces of paper and put the class in small groups to write their own messages. Monitor and offer help as necessary.

At the end of the writing phase, elicit sentences from different groups and build up a class answer on the board. Remind the students to write the date and, if they sign their name in *kanji,* to write it in English underneath. Addresses might also be written in thank-you cards. Suggest to students that personal messages, such as the *Thank you for …-ing* and *I really enjoyed …* are appropriate in thank-you cards.

Special messages for classmates

If the class is going to disband at the end of this course, spend some time having the classmates thank each other. There are many ways to set up thank-you activities. Here are a few ideas:

Taped messages

Students write their name on a piece of paper. These are redistributed to the other students. Each student looks at the paper he/she has been given and records onto a class cassette a personal message to the named person. Play the final product with messages to everyone (and a message to the group from yourself, if you like) in your final lesson with the group.

Message boards

Give the class a set amount of time (20 minutes should be enough) to go around the class and write a short thank-you message in English in the back cover of their classmates' textbook.

For weaker groups, write some examples on the board first to give the class ideas to get them started, e.g., *Good luck in your job! / I'll miss you! / Thank you for helping me with my homework! / Let's keep in touch.*

Find someone who you want to thank for…

Elicit ideas and write a list similar to this on the board:

> *Thank you for…*
> *… helping me with my homework.*
> *… being my partner in "Passport" lessons.*
> *… always wearing such great clothes!*

Tell the class to stand up. Give them a short time limit and tell them to thank as many people in the room as they can. If someone thanks them for something, they should of course thank them back. (Bear in mind that this activity is really effective only with groups that have enjoyed working together!)

Activity

New partners. Read the instructions aloud and allocate roles. When the students are ready to start, have them close their books. Monitor the activity and give feedback at the end. Write some of the more important errors you heard on the board and ask the students to correct them.

Ask some pairs to perform their role-play for the rest of the class.

Finishing the lesson

Bring the class back together and congratulate them on their efforts. Tell the students to look again at the Background notes for Unit 19. List the functions on the board and elicit an example for each one. Write the examples too, e.g.:

Saying goodbye:
Goodbye. I'll miss you.

Expressing your thanks:
Thank you for everything.

Giving and receiving gifts:
This is for you. It's from Japan.
Oh, you shouldn't have!

Expressing wishes for the future:
I hope to see you again someday.

Ask the class to copy down the examples. Assign any review homework you feel is necessary. Tell the class that in the next lesson they will learn how to check in at a foreign airport.

Ask the class to read the *Background notes* for Unit 20 before the next class.

Optional Activity

Review: giving gifts from Japan

Draw simple pictures on the board, or bring in real items if you have them, of things that could be suitable Japanese gifts for a host family or friend overseas. Put the students in small groups. Ask them to practice in their groups what they would say when giving each of the gifts, and how they would answer the question: *What is it?*

After giving the groups time to practice using all the items, nominate some groups to listen to their replies and write some of the responses on the board. Example ideas for gifts and possible definitions:

sake: *This is Japanese rice wine. You can drink it hot or cold. It's delicious, but it's very strong, so only drink a little at a time!*

washi paper doll mobile: *washi is Japanese paper. This is a mobile to hang up somewhere in the house!*

a fan: *This is a traditional Japanese fan. This one is made of sandalwood so it smells really nice when you open it. You can use it in the summer!*

a windchime: *I think you have these in this country too. It's a traditional Japanese windchime. You can hang it outside your window in the spring or summer, and it makes a gentle sound as the wind blows.*

5- or 50-yen coins: *These are really small coins in Japan, but I thought your children would like to have some. They are quite unusual because they have holes in the center of the coin.*

Unit 20
How many bags do you have?

Topic / functions

Asking where to check in

Saying where you want to sit

Finding out about the flight

Review

Saying goodbye

Books closed. Write these scrambled sentences on the board and ask the students to work in pairs to decode them.

1 stay my enjoyed I really
2 for goodbye to me Please Steve say
3 for Thanks everything
4 hope see I again to you sometime
5 address my is This
6 touch Let's in keep

Elicit the answers and write them on the board.

Answers:

1 I really enjoyed my stay.
2 Please say goodbye to Steve for me.
3 Thanks for everything.
4 I hope to see you again sometime.
5 This is my address.
6 Let's keep in touch.

Warming up

Preview: Background notes for Unit 20

Books closed. Remind the students about the background reading they did for Unit 20. Elicit the names of different parts of the airport and write them up randomly on the board. Tell the students to work in pairs and put the places in order, according to which one you visit first, second, and so on, when catching a flight. For example:

check-in counter → security check →

passport control → duty-free shopping area →

departure lounge → the plane

Optional Activity

Scrambled words

Put a list of scrambled words on the board and do the first one as an example. Ask the students to work in pairs to unscramble the words. The first pair to finish is the winner!

Vocabulary used at the check-in counter:

1 saiv
2 comyeno lassc
3 ssapptro
4 ketcit
5 liase teas
6 gugglae
7 ginbroad drac
8 neymo

Answers:

1 (a) visa
2 economy class
3 (a) passport
4 (a) ticket
5 (an) aisle seat
6 luggage
7 (a) boarding card
8 money

Open your books

Tell the students to look at the picture on p. 50. Remind the students that Rie and Miki are going to travel to Canada from the U.S. before going home to Japan. Ask some general questions about the picture to elicit extra vocabulary: *What is Rie doing? What's his job?* etc. Read the caption aloud: *Rie is checking in for a flight from San Francisco to Vancouver.*

Listening

Read the instructions aloud. Pre-teach *aisle seat*, *gate*, and *luggage* before starting. Read the sentences. When everyone is ready, play the cassette and monitor to check that everyone is completing the task. Tell the students: *Work in pairs. Check your answers together. Do you have the same answers?*

Say: *Now listen again.* Replay the cassette, if necessary, pausing after the key sentences (e.g., *I'd like an aisle seat, please.*).

Tell the students to check in pairs again. Play the tape one more time and elicit the answers by taking a class vote. Write the answers on the board.

Answers:
1 an aisle seat
2 Gate 18
3 DL 1618
4 four items of luggage

Look and learn

Books closed. Draw a stick picture on the board of a check-in clerk and a passenger and point to them as you drill the language study, to indicate to the students who is speaking. You may need to explain *scales* again (the students met the word in unit 16) as well as *prefer*, *on time*, and *cabin*. After drilling the questions and answers, have the students open their books to p. 50 and practice in pairs.

Conversation

Hold your book so that the students can see p. 51. Say: *Look at page 51. Look at the "Conversation."* Read the instructions aloud and point to the picture of Rie on p. 50 again to remind the students what she is doing. Play the cassette through once and have the students check together in pairs. Replay the conversation, pausing after each blank to give the students time to check their answers and change any information they couldn't catch the first time. If your class is struggling, replay the key parts again. Let the class check their answers in pairs. Elicit the answers and write them on the board.

Answers:
1 DL 1618
2 Non-smoking
3 yes, please
4 two suitcases
5 Gate 16

Books closed. Model the conversation, or use the cassette, drilling chorally. Model the numbers and the *w* sound in *would you* carefully. After sufficient practice have the students open their books again to p. 51 to practice the conversation in pairs, using the "read, look up, and speak" technique.

Over to you!

New pairs. Read the instructions and have the students practice the new dialogs. Students who cope easily should be encouraged to cover the conversation and make new ones using only the prompts. Monitor and give feedback on any problem areas at the end. Ask some students to perform their conversations for the rest of the group.

Optional Activity

Luggage labels

Writing Japanese home addresses in English can be very difficult for students. Draw an outline of a luggage label on the board and write the address of the institution where you are teaching in English, in order to show the class the order for writing addresses (i.e., name, street number, street name, town, city, area, zip/post code). Remind the class that when they travel, they should put their address both in Japan and in the country they are visiting inside each bag as well as on a label on the outside, and preferably in both Japanese and English. Having address and name labels written in English may speed things up slightly should a bag go missing abroad.

Tell the students to copy the outline of the label and to practice writing their own name and address, in English. Monitor and offer help as necessary.

Activity

New partners. Read the instructions and allocate roles. If possible, move chairs and desks and set the classroom up to represent airport check-in counters. When the students are ready, have them visit the check-in counters and act out their conversations. If you like, tell the travelers to use their textbook to represent their passport and to check the bags they have with them in the classroom.

After trying out the conversation, tell the tourists to repeat the conversation at a different counter. Encourage several repetitions until they can cope well. Remind the class to use emergency language when they don't understand something. Halfway through, have the students change roles.

At the end, give feedback on any important errors you heard. Nominate some pairs to act out their conversations for the rest of the group.

Optional Activities

Finding out about flights

For weaker groups, brainstorm a "departure board" and write the information on the board under these headings:

Flight number	To	Scheduled time of departure	Status
BA17	Osaka	14:00	Boarding at Gate 25
QF21	Tokyo	14:35	Last call

Ask some general questions to a few students to give the class a chance to understand the chart, e.g., *Which flight goes to Osaka? Which gate does it leave from? What time does it leave?* Put the students in small groups and have them ask questions and give answers about the departure board. Tell the student to ask six questions each.

Low-level groups find question formation very difficult. This task is reassuring as all the information is provided, and the fact that they are working in small groups is less threatening.

Future study plans

If your class is disbanding after finishing the book, some students may be uncertain how best to continue their studies. Spend a few minutes talking with the group about their English language learning plans after the course, and offer help and information as necessary. If your students will be traveling overseas soon, make sure they have your home or school address for postcards!

About *Passport*: Feedback

If you have time in your schedule, it is always interesting to get feedback from the students on how they coped with the course and what they felt about the materials. Hand out paper to the students and tell them not to write their names on the paper. Higher-level classes can be told to write their feedback notes about the course without much guidance, but weaker groups do better if given specific questions to answer, e.g., *Which unit did you like best? Which was the most useful / boring / fun / difficult / easy? What do you like about "Passport"? What do you dislike?*

Be careful when you set up this activity to tell the students exactly what you want them to comment on, or they may believe they are completing evaluation forms for your superiors regarding your teaching, in which case you will only receive notes which basically thank you for your nice lessons.

Finishing the lesson

Bring the class together and congratulate them for their efforts. Tell the students to look again at the *Background notes* for Unit 20. List the functions on the board and elicit an example for each one. Write the examples too, e.g.:

Asking where to check in:
  Can I check in here for Flight BA 351?

Saying where you want to sit:
  I'd like a window seat, please.

Finding out about the flight:
  Which gate is it?

Ask the class to copy down the examples. Assign any review homework you feel is necessary. Congratulate the group on finishing all twenty units and tell them that in their final lesson using *Passport*, they will play a game called *The Survival Game!*. Suggest to the class that they spend some time looking again at the *Look and learn* sections in each unit for a few minutes before the next class.

Optional Activity

Checking in: matching the questions and answers

Write the following questions and answers on the board. Tell the students to work in pairs and match them. Elicit the answers and have the students practice together.

The questions:

1 May I see your ticket and passport, please?
2 Do you have any carry-on luggage?
3 Did you pack these bags yourself?
4 Which gate is it?
5 Could I have a window seat, please?

The answers:

a Yes, I did.
b Number 40.
c I'll just check the computer.
d Here you are.
e Just this one.

Answers: 1 d 2 e 3 a 4 b 5 c

The Survival Game!

This game (pp. 52-57 of the Student Book) is a review game for the entire coursebook and is designed to be a fun and lively classroom activity for the students to play in small groups. Spend a few minutes before class going through the rules on page 52 to ensure that you are clear about how to play the game! Take in a coin for each group, in case the students don't have any money on them. It's a nice touch to take in currency from your own country, if you have coins to hand (British coins, for instance, do have a "head" - the Queen's - on them, unlike Japanese ones). If you have counters available, take these in too, although the students can use small pieces of paper with their initials written on them instead. In class, demonstrate how to flip a coin and tell the class that "heads or tails" is a common way of deciding things, in much the same way as the Japanese use the "paper - scissors - stone" game.

Set the game up slowly by putting the class into groups of four or six students, checking that each pair has one book open at the board (pp. 56-57) and another open at the dialog pages. Each group consists of pairs of A and B students: check that the students know who their partner is and whether they are Student A or Student B. Tell the students that one pair is a team and that each team has one counter. The first team to travel around the board and back to Japan is the winning team.

Tell the students to read the instructions. They are quite complex for learners at this level, so give them a few minutes to get the general idea. Hand out coins and counters, or ask the students to find their own.

Demonstrate how the game is played by taking the place of a student in a group: flip a coin, move your counter the appropriate number of spaces (Heads = 1, Tails = 2) and ask your partner to read the cues aloud so that you are seen to be thinking up replies. Respond clearly, enthusiastically and try to make eye contact with your partner where possible. Do not look at the book. The class will catch on very quickly at this point and be keen to start, so read the first part of the instructions aloud to the group, say "Have a good trip!" and let them proceed.

Your role during the game is to be available for help, iron out any misunderstandings that might occur during the first few minutes, and act as a roving monitor to see how they are getting on. Ensure that the teams take turns, that each team is aware that his/her partner is not in competition with him/her, and that when the cues are read aloud, the responding partner is not also reading the text but only listening. As the game progresses, insist that the students make eye contact with each other when they hold the conversation (they should be well-versed in the "read, look up and speak" technique by now!): higher-level groups should act out these dialogs with as much realism as they can muster.

If any of the dialogs proves too demanding, point out to teams who need help that the number on each square corresponds to the unit in book, and if they are really stuck they can look back at the "Conversation" in that unit for help. Encourage the students to perform their roles and congratulate them where possible: the aim of this game is to leave each students with the strong impression that although they are of course going to make mistakes, they clearly do have enough English to survive overseas and are able to make themselves understood. The atmosphere in the classroom at this point should be extremely positive!

Some groups will finish before others: tell these groups to spend a few moments looking at the dialogs they didn't do while the rest of the groups finish the game. Bring the class back together and congratulate them on their efforts. Tell them that in your opinion, they are more than ready to start using their passports and go traveling!

Photocopiable Material

This section contains the material for the optional activities referred to throughout this Teacher's Guide, and tapescripts of the recorded material in the Student Book. These pages may be photocopied.

For the photocopiable activity pages, the unit number and reference for the page in this Teacher's Guide containing the relevant instructions are supplied.

Photocopiable page A (Unit 2, see p. 16)

Photocopiable page B

(Unit 2, see p. 18)

Adapted from the I-94 form, which visitors to the U.S. have to complete.

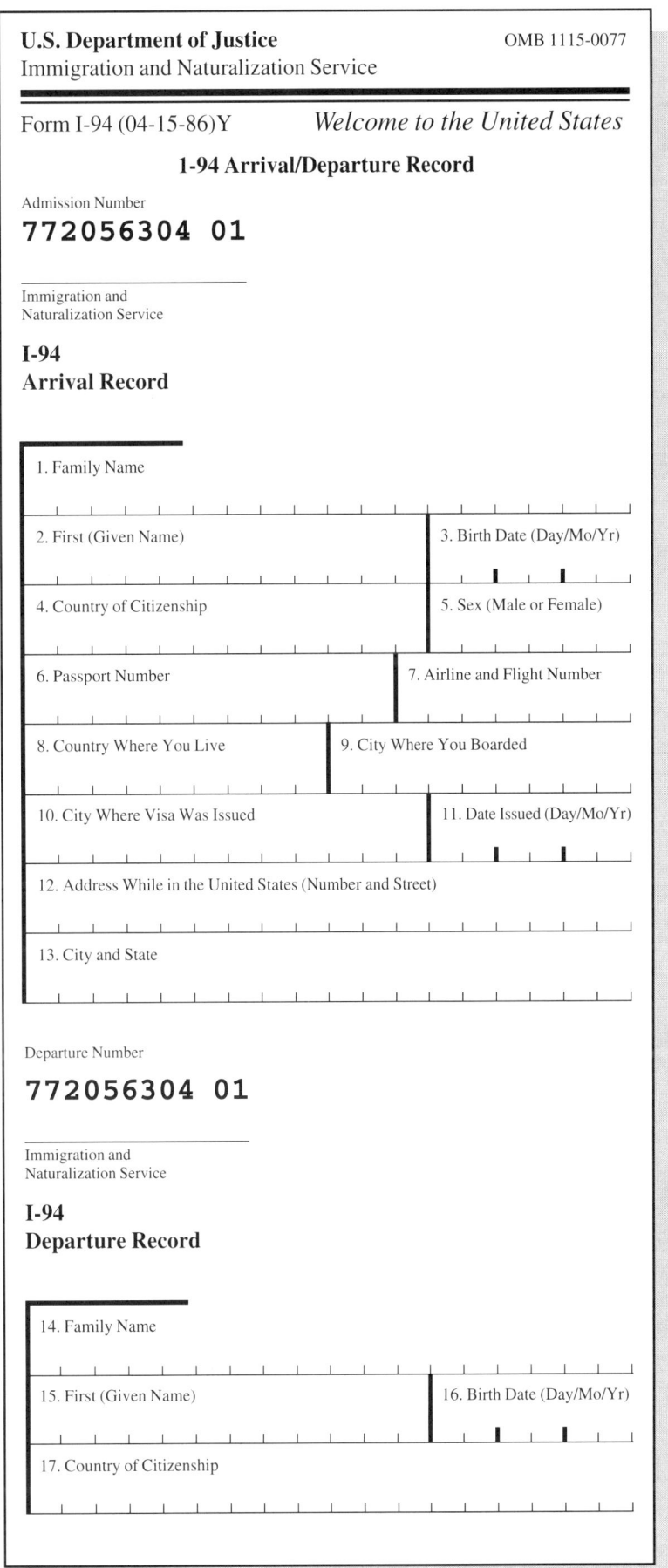

U.S. Department of Justice   OMB 1115-0077
Immigration and Naturalization Service

Form I-94 (04-15-86)Y   *Welcome to the United States*

1-94 Arrival/Departure Record

Admission Number

772056304 01

Immigration and
Naturalization Service

**I-94
Arrival Record**

1. Family Name

2. First (Given Name)   3. Birth Date (Day/Mo/Yr)

4. Country of Citizenship   5. Sex (Male or Female)

6. Passport Number   7. Airline and Flight Number

8. Country Where You Live   9. City Where You Boarded

10. City Where Visa Was Issued   11. Date Issued (Day/Mo/Yr)

12. Address While in the United States (Number and Street)

13. City and State

Departure Number

772056304 01

Immigration and
Naturalization Service

**I-94
Departure Record**

14. Family Name

15. First (Given Name)   16. Birth Date (Day/Mo/Yr)

17. Country of Citizenship

Photocopiable page C

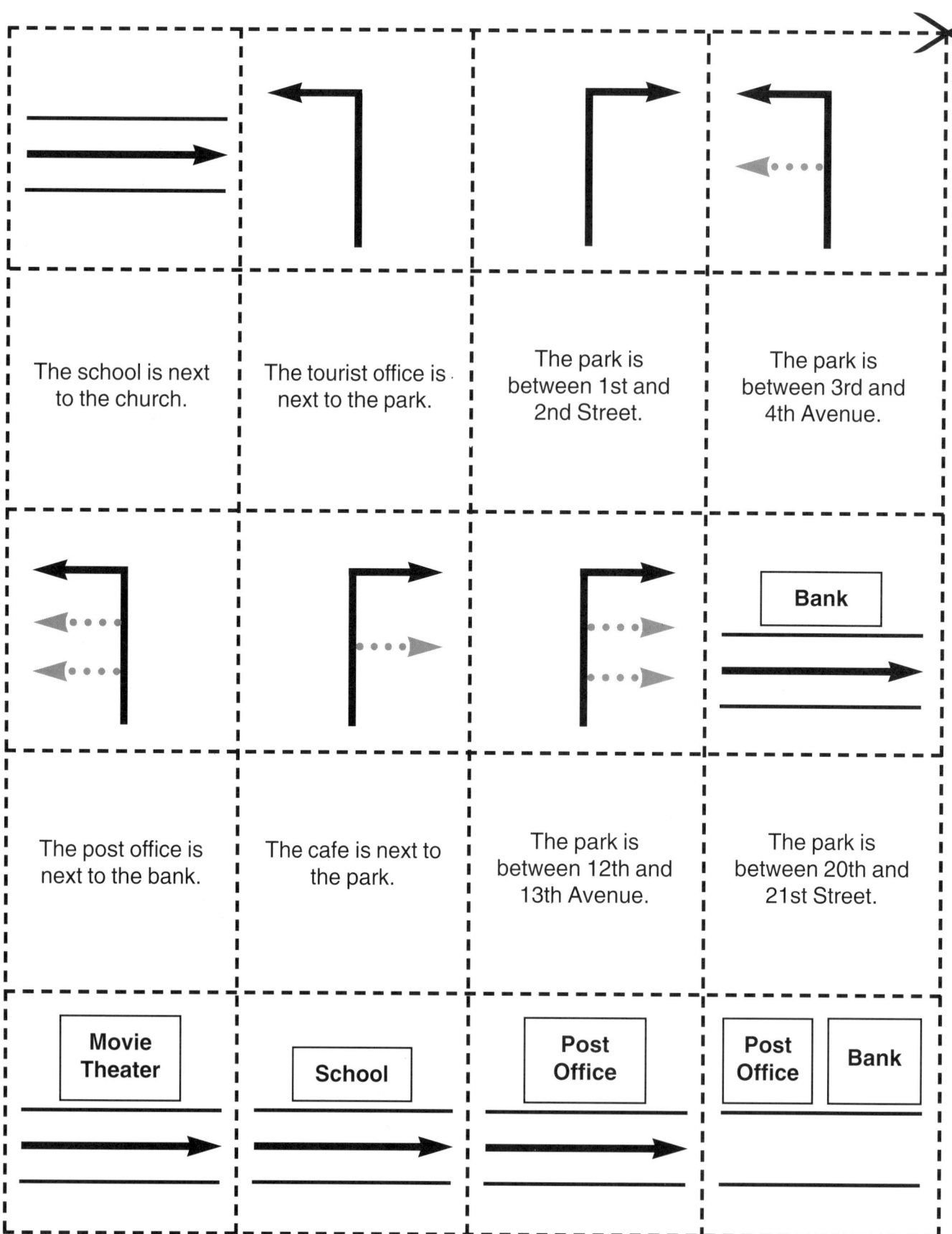

The school is next to the church.

The tourist office is next to the park.

The park is between 1st and 2nd Street.

The park is between 3rd and 4th Avenue.

Bank

The post office is next to the bank.

The cafe is next to the park.

The park is between 12th and 13th Avenue.

The park is between 20th and 21st Street.

Movie Theater

School

Post Office

Post Office

Bank

Photocopiable page D (Unit 5, see p. 27)

Go straight on.	Turn left.	Turn right.	Take the second left.
House **Bank**	**School** **Church**	**Tourist Office** **Park**	20th Street **Park** 21st Street
Take the second right.	Take the third left.	Take the third right.	Go past the movie theater.
Cafe **Park**	12th Avenue **Park** 13th Avenue	1st Street **Park** 2nd Street	3rd Avenue **Park** 4th Avenue
Go past the bank.	Go past the school.	Go past the post office.	The house is next to the bank.

Photocopiable page E (Unit 5, see p. 28)

Student A. Read Look and learn on page 14 again. Do not look at Student B's map.
Take turns. Ask where these places are and write them on the map:

- the movie theater
- the tourist information office
- the hairdressers
- the taxi stand
- the discount record store
- the sports shop
- the flower shop
- the library

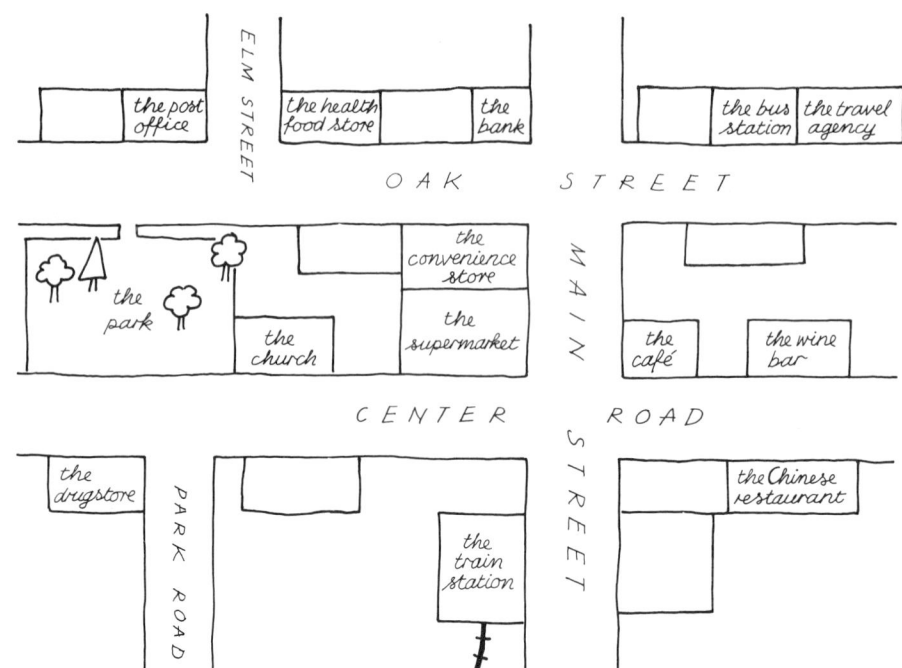

Student B. Read Look and learn on page 14 again. Do not look at Student A's map.
Take turns. Ask where these places are and write them on the map:

- the supermarket
- the Chinese restaurant
- the convenience store
- the health food store
- the wine bar
- the drugstore
- the travel agency
- the post office

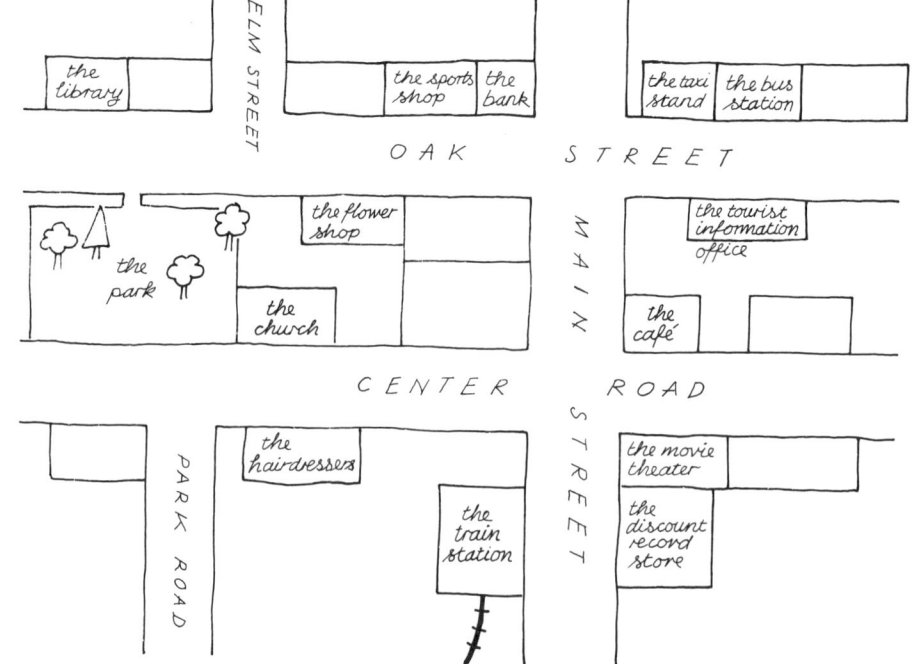

Photocopiable page F (Unit 6, see p. 32)

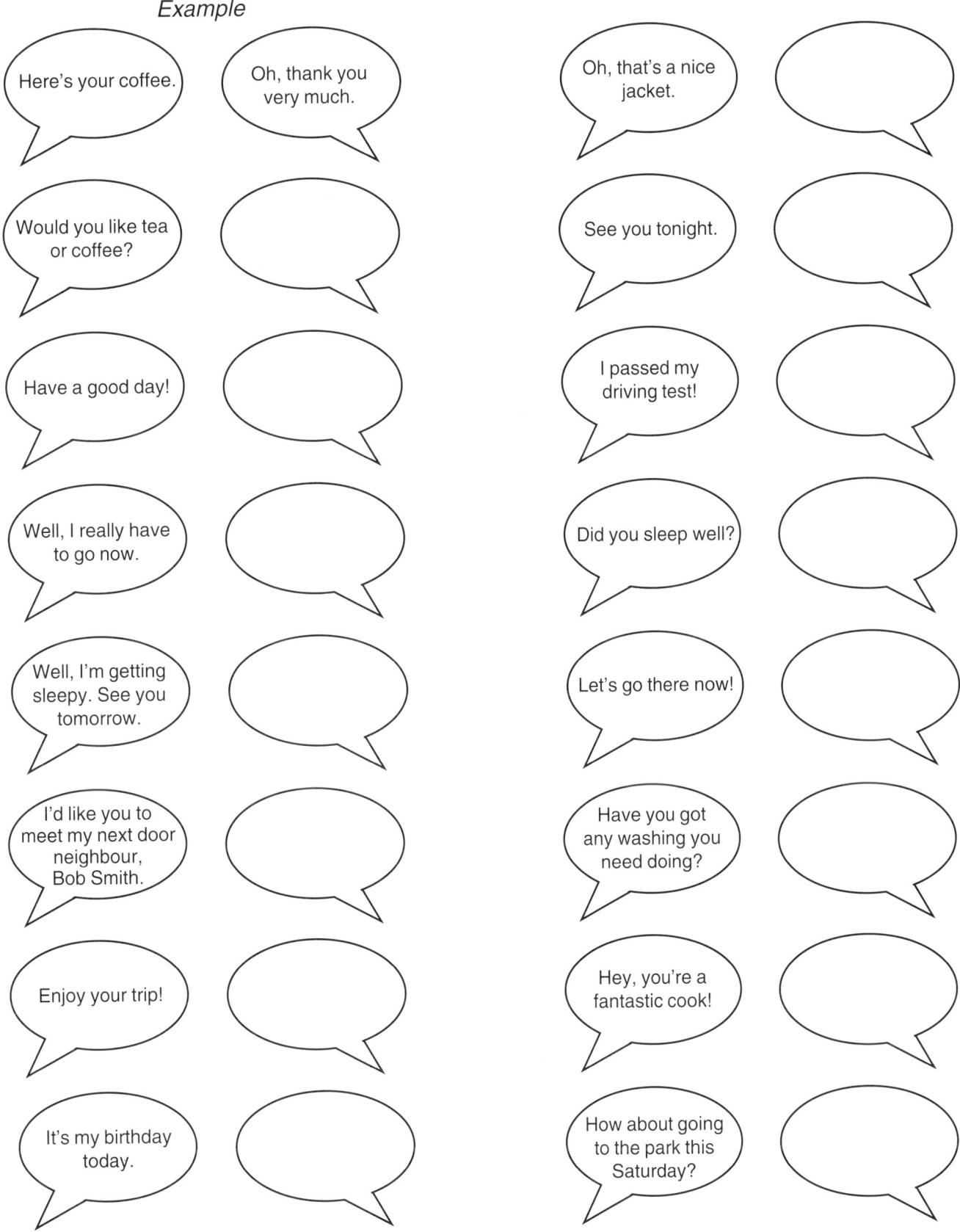

Example

Here's your coffee.

Oh, thank you very much.

Oh, that's a nice jacket.

Would you like tea or coffee?

See you tonight.

Have a good day!

I passed my driving test!

Well, I really have to go now.

Did you sleep well?

Well, I'm getting sleepy. See you tomorrow.

Let's go there now!

I'd like you to meet my next door neighbour, Bob Smith.

Have you got any washing you need doing?

Enjoy your trip!

Hey, you're a fantastic cook!

It's my birthday today.

How about going to the park this Saturday?

Photocopiable page G (Unit 7, see p. 34)

I went skiing yesterday. But I crashed! I can't walk very well today. *(My leg hurts.)*	I went to a birthday party yesterday. There was so much food! I ate for about four hours! *(I have a stomachache.)*
I went to a party last night. I drank too much beer! I feel terrible this morning. *(I have a headache.)*	I've been using a computer for the last eight hours. *(My eyes hurt.)*
I went to a very noisy rock concert last night. It was so loud! *(I have an earache.)*	My car wouldn't start yesterday. I had to push it! *(I have a backache.)*
I went to karaoke last night with my friends. I sang for three hours! I can't speak very well today. *(I have a sore throat.)*	I've been foolish. I haven't been to the dentist for three years and I feel terrible now! *(I have a toothache.)*
I went camping yesterday. It rained and snowed, and I couldn't make a fire to keep warm. *(I have a cold.)*	I feel hot and strange. I think I should go home to bed right now. *(I have a fever.)*

Photocopiable page H (Unit 8, see p. 38)

✂

Hello. Could I speak to Koji Watanabe, please?

This is Koji. Is that Pete?

Yeah, how are you doing?

I'm fine, thanks. And you?

Good, thanks. Listen, are you busy on Saturday night?

No, I don't think so. Why?

Well, there's a party at Mike's place. Do you want to go?

Sounds great! What time should we meet?

I thought we could go for a drink first, so let's meet at 8:30
in the Red Oak pub.

8:30? Ok, great! See you then. Thanks, Pete.

No worries. See you on Saturday.

'Bye.

Photocopiable page I (Unit 8, see p. 38)

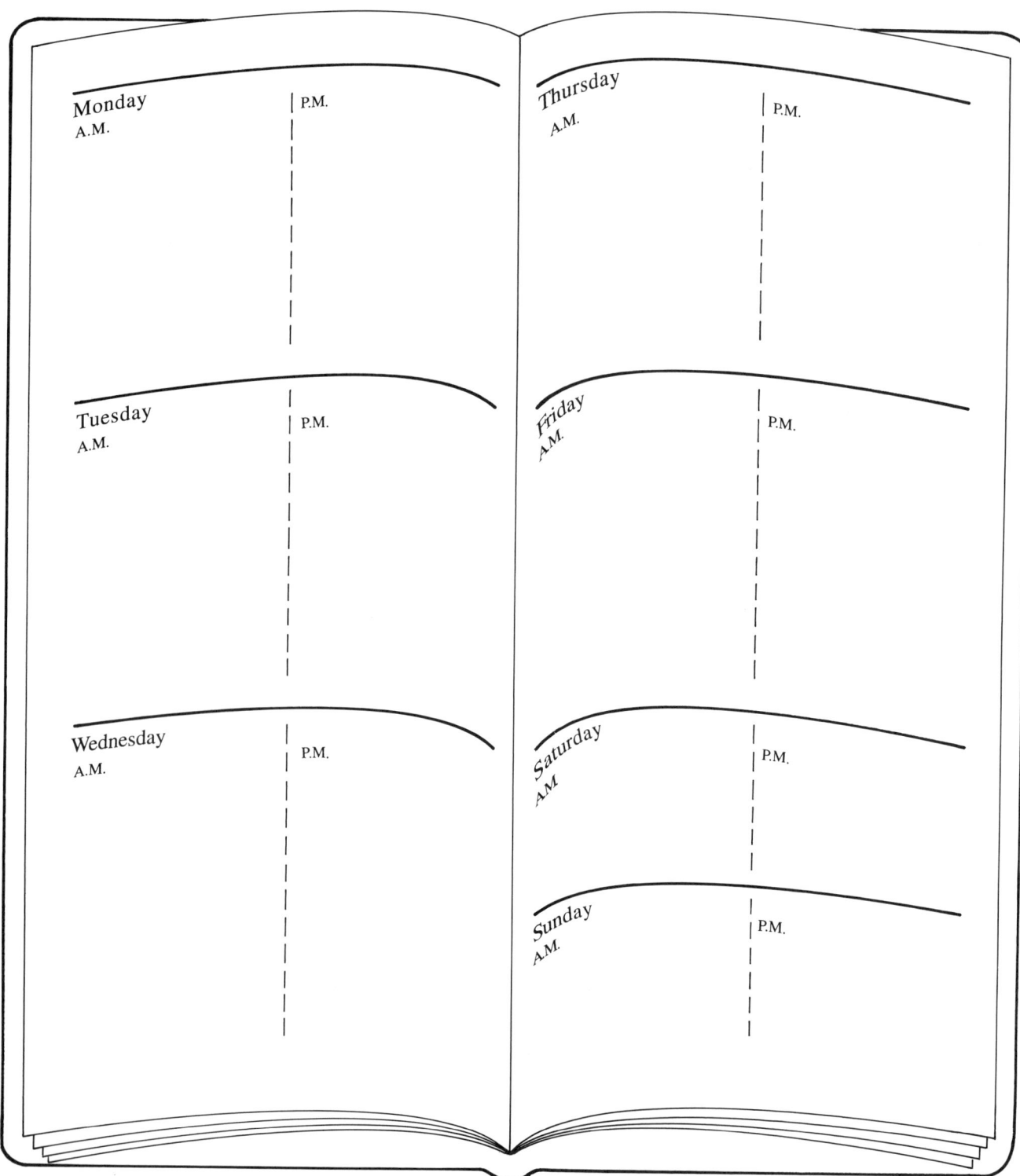

Photocopiable page J (Unit 9, see p. 40)

Invitations

Find someone who is free. Fix a time and a meeting place.

Invite a classmate to the movies.

....

Invite a classmate to a party.

....

Invite a classmate to coffee after class.

....

Invite a classmate to dinner this week.

....

Invite a classmate to go shopping sometime this weekend.

....

Invite a classmate to go to karaoke with you.

....

Invite a classmate out to lunch today.

....

Invite a classmate out to do something on Friday night.

....

FREE QUESTION!

....

Photocopiable page K (Units 1–10, see p. 47)

START →

1
Would you like
chicken or fish?

1
Could I have
a newspaper,
please?

2
What's the purpose
of your visit?

2
What's your
occupation?

2
Where are you
from?

**FREE
QUESTION!**

3
Say these numbers:
1,500
15,000
150,000
1,500,000

3
What's the
exchange rate
today?

4
Could you
spell your name,
please?

4
What time
will you arrive at
the hotel?

FREE QUESTION!

8
Are you busy
on Saturday?

8
Tell me ten parts
of the body.

7
How do you feel?

6
Could you show
me how to use the
washing machine?

6
Is it OK if I call
my mother today?

6
Do you mind
if I smoke?

5
Where is the
nearest post office?

**FREE
QUESTION!**

5
Excuse me.
Where is the
nearest station?

4
Would you like
a single or a
double?

8
Can you make it
for dinner on
Thursday?

8
Where should
we meet?

9
Are you ready
to order?

9
What would
you like for
dessert?

9
Would you
like something
to drink?

10
Do you have
any brothers
and sisters?

**FREE
QUESTION!**

10
What do you
usually do on
weekends?

Tell me about
your family.

FINISH

Photocopiable page L (Unit 11, see p. 48)

Finding out about ....

animals	famous cities to visit	tallest building ....
plants	typical food	best place to go on a Saturday night ....
flag design	famous landmarks	best beach ....
religions	major airline companies	coldest city ....
popular sports	major newspapers	capital city ....
prime minister	cost of local stamps	national holidays ....
wettest month	currency and kinds of coin	brands of beer ....
driest month and average temperature	store opening hours	best place to live ....

Photocopiable page M (Unit 12, see pp. 50–51)

be was been	**cost** cost cost	**find** found found
begin began begun	**do** did done	**fly** flew flown
bring brought brought	**drink** drank drunk	**forget** forgot forgotten
buy bought bought	**drive** drove driven	**get** got gotten
choose chose chosen	**eat** ate eaten	**go** went gone

Photocopiable page N (Unit 12, see pp. 50–51)

have had had	**meet** met met	**speak** spoke spoken
know knew known	**say** said said	**swim** swam swum
leave left left	**see** saw seen	**take** took taken
lose lost lost	**sing** sang sung	**wear** wore worn
make made made	**sleep** slept slept	**write** wrote written

Photocopiable page O (Unit 15, see p. 61)

to a "J - League" soccer game	to a disco	to a "pyjama party"
to a party	shopping	swimming
on a mountain walk	to a fireworks show	to Hawaii
to work at McDonalds	on a picnic	skiing
to Disneyland	to an interview	to an expensive restaurant
to a wedding	to a fancy-dress party	on a long plane trip
scuba-diving	on a river cruise	to a sports center
to the beach	on a date	bowling

Photocopiable page P (Unit 17, see p. 67)

Student B (Tourist.)

: …

Yes, please. I'd like to book two tickets for a West End show, please.

: …

Um, I'd like two seats for ……………, please.

: …

I'd like to go on (day and date) …………… , please.

: …

The …………… , please.

: …

That's fine. I'd like to pay by …………… card, please.

: …

Yes, my name is …………… and my card number is ……………

: …

Thank you very much. Goodbye!

Student A (Theater ticket agency clerk.)

Hello. Low-cost Ticket Agency. May I help you?

: …

Yes, and which show was that? We have tickets available for Cats, Les Miserables, Miss Saigon, Phantom of the Opera, and many more!

: …

I see. Which day do you want to go?

: …

Is that the matinée or evening performance?

: …

Fine. I have two seats in the …………… . They're £…………… each.

: …

Can I have your name and card number, please?

: …

Thank you Mr./Ms. …………… . Please collect your tickets 30 minutes before the performance at the theater.

: …

Photocopiable page Q (Unit 18, see p. 70)

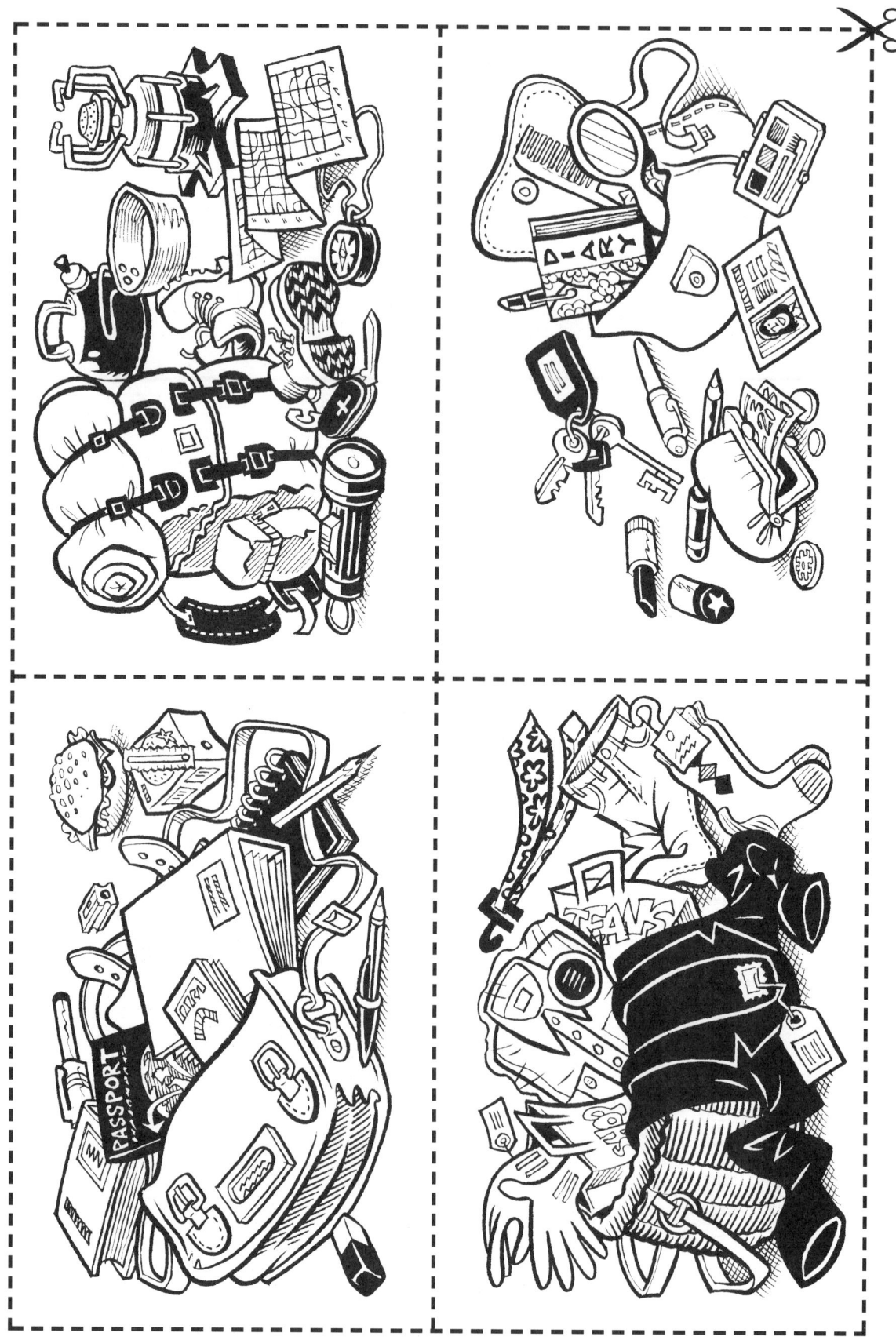

Photocopiable page R (Unit 18, see p. 70)

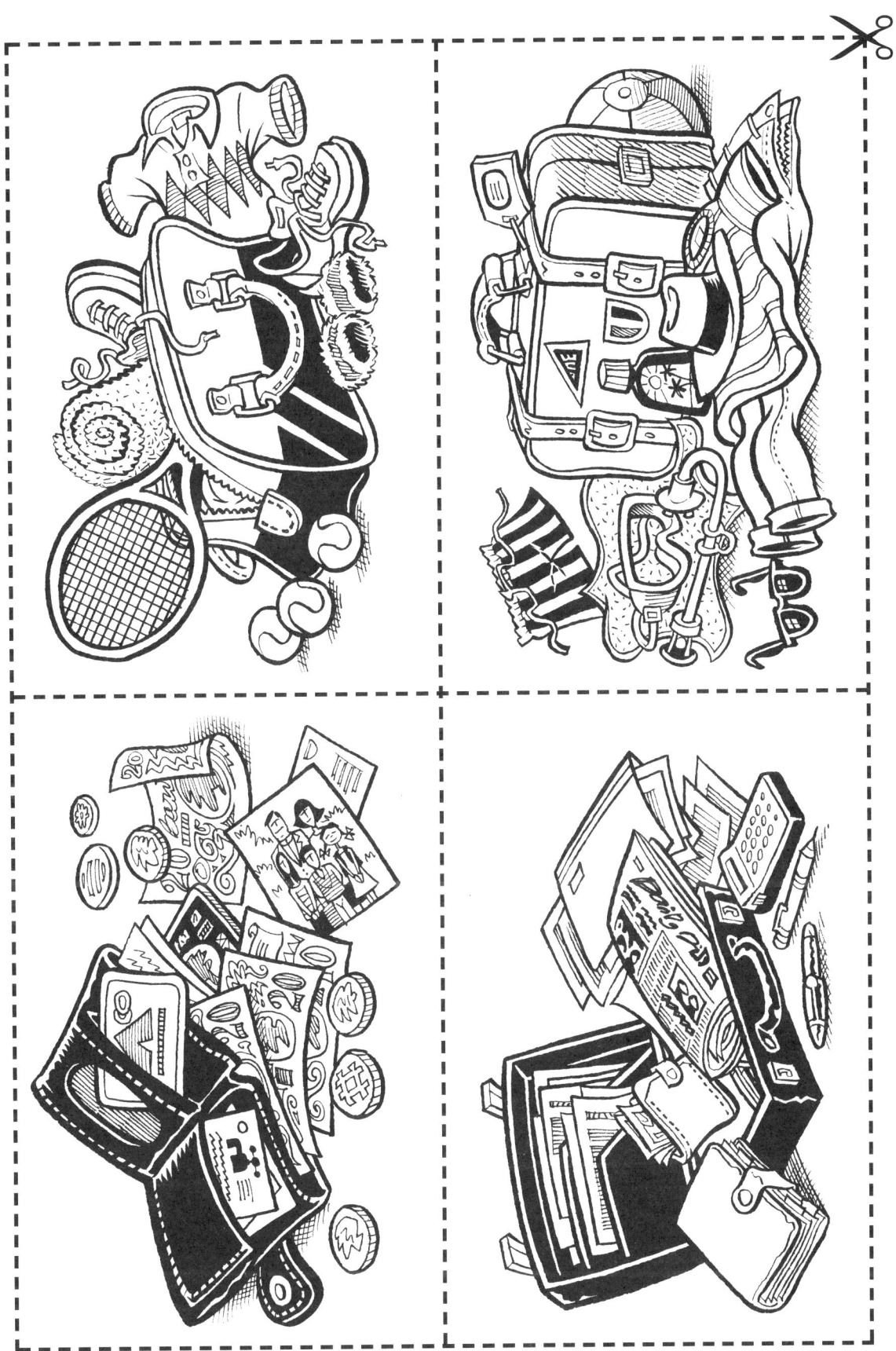

Tapescripts

Unit 1 Would you like beef or fish?

Listening

What does each person want? Listen. Check the correct answer.

Conversation 1: Miki

Attendant: And what would you like to drink?
Miki: Excuse me? Could you repeat that, please?
Attendant: To drink. Anything to drink?
Miki: Mm. Yes, please. May I have, er …?
Attendant: We have fruit juices, soda, wine, beer …
Miki: I'd like some wine later. But now, I'd like er …
Attendant: Orange juice?
Miki: Er, no. Apple juice, please!
Attendant: Sure, here you are.

Conversation 2: Rie

Attendant: Did you see the menu?
Rie: Menu? I'm sorry, I don't understand.
Attendant: What would you like to eat? We have beef or fish.
Rie: Ah! Yes, please.
Attendant: Er, which would you like?
Rie: Oh, sorry! It's my English.
Attendant: No problem. We have beef or fish.
Rie: Er, not fish, please … Beef?
Attendant: OK. Beef it is! Here you are.
Rie: Thank you very much.

Conversation 3: Koji

Attendant: Hello!
Koji: Oh, hello!
Attendant: Would you like tea or coffee?
Koji: The tea – is it very strong?
Attendant: Well, yes, it is.
Koji: OK. Then I'll have coffee. I don't like strong tea.
Attendant: No problem. Could you pass me your cup, please?

Conversation 4: Mayumi

Attendant: Yes, madam. How may I help you?
Mayumi: Um, I'd like … um, I'm sorry, I don't know the word … It's for sleeping.
Attendant: Ah, a blanket? You'd like a blanket?
Mayumi: No, not a blanket. For my head.
Attendant: Ah, right! A pillow! There's one up here, I think … Yes, here you are.
Mayumi: Oh, thanks.
Attendant: Have a pleasant rest.
Mayumi: Thank you very much.

Conversation 5: Makoto

Attendant: Hello, sir.
Makoto: Oh, hello.

Attendant: Would you like a newspaper, sir? We have English and Japanese newspapers.
Makoto: Er, could you say that more slowly, please?
Attendant: Yes, sir. Would you like an English newspaper or a Japanese newspaper?
Makoto: May I have an English newspaper, please?
Attendant: An English newspaper? We do have some Japanese ones.
Makoto: Oh, no! An English newspaper! I have to practice my English!
Attendant: Ah, I see. OK.

Conversation

Listen to this conversation between Koji and a flight attendant. Fill in the blanks.

Attendant: Would you like chicken or fish?
Koji: I'd like fish, please.
Attendant: Here you are.
Koji: Thank you.
Attendant: And would you like some wine?
Koji: I'm sorry, I don't understand. Could you repeat that, please?
Attendant: Would you like some wine?
Koji: No, thank you. But may I have a beer, please?
Attendant: Certainly. Here you are.
Koji: Thank you very much.

Unit 2 Can I have your passport, please?

Listening

Rie is talking to an American immigration officer. Listen. Circle T (true) or F (false).

Conversation 1

Officer: Next, please!
Rie: Good morning.
Officer: Yes. Good afternoon!
Rie: Oh, er, sorry. Good afternoon!
Officer: And you're from Japan?
Rie: Yes.

Conversation 2

Officer: OK. Do you have your I-ninety-four?
Rie: Excuse me? I …?
Officer: Your white form for immigration … Your landing card?
Rie: Oh, this one?
Officer: Yes, that's right. That's your I-ninety-four.
Rie: Sorry!
Officer: Yes, I need that, please.
Rie: Oh, OK. Here you are!

Conversation 3

Officer: And the purpose of your visit?
Rie: Sorry, I don't understand.
Officer: Your visit here. Why are you here? … Business or pleasure?
Rie: Business? No. This is my vacation.
Officer: Vacation. Fine. That's what I need to know. Purpose of visit: pleasure! Thank you.

Conversation 4

Officer: And your occupation.
Rie: Oh, yes. My job?
Officer: Yes, your job.
Rie: I'm a college student, but I also work in a restaurant.
Officer: You work full-time in a restaurant?
Rie: No, I'm a student. I only work part-time in the restaurant.
Officer: I see. So you're a college student.
Rie: Yes, that's right.

Conversation 5

Officer: And your address?
Rie: In Japan?
Officer: No. Excuse me. Your address in the States.
Rie: It's a hotel. The Hotel Gorham.
Officer: The Hotel Gorham? Is that on West Fifty-sixth Street?
Rie: Yes, I think so … No, wait! I think it's on West Fifty-fifth Street.
Officer: OK. The Hotel Gorham on West Fifty-fifth Street.

Conversation 6

Officer: And will you be there all vacation?
Rie: All vacation? No. We're going to travel a lot.
Officer: In the U.S. only?
Rie: The U.S., yes. And Vancouver.
Officer: Vancouver. So you're going to Canada, also?
Rie: Yes.

Conversation 7

Officer: And how long will your trip last?
Rie: Sorry? Could you repeat that, please?
Officer: Er, how long will you be here? One month? … Two months?
Rie: Six weeks.
Officer: OK. Thanks.

Conversation 8

Officer: And one last question. About money.
Rie: Er, do you want money?
Officer: No, no, no! But I need to know how much money – cash – you have.
Rie: Oh, I'm not sure exactly.
Officer: A thousand dollars?
Rie: Um, yes, no. Fifteen hundred.
Officer: Fine. That's all. Thank you very much, ma'am. Arigato gozaimasu.
Rie: Hee? (*Japanese expression of surprise*) You can speak Japanese?
Officer: Just a little. You learn some doing this job. Next, please!

Conversation

Listen and check your answers.

Officer: May I see your passport and your I-ninety-four, please?
Miki: Yes. Here they are.
Officer: Thank you. What's your job in Japan?
Miki: I'm a college student.
Officer: What's the purpose of your visit?
Miki: Well, I'm going sightseeing.
Officer: Are you traveling alone?
Miki: No, with my friend, Rie Yasuda.
Officer: What's your address in the U.S.?
Miki: It's the Hotel Gorham on West Fifty-fifth Street.
Officer: And how long are you intending to stay?
Miki: For six weeks.
Officer: That's fine, thank you. Next, please!

Unit 3 Can I change some money here?

Listening

Listen. Check the amount of money you hear.

Conversation 1: Koji is asking about an English course.

Woman: Community College. How can I help you?
Koji: Hello. Yes, how much is your intensive English course, please?
Woman: Well, how many weeks would you like to study?
Koji: Er, two months, so eight weeks.
Woman: Let's see. That would be four thousand dollars.
Koji: Four thousand dollars? OK. Thank you.
Woman: Thank you. Bye.
Koji: Bye. … Four thousand dollars!

Conversation 2: Rie is buying a camera.

Woman: Good morning. Can I help you?
Rie: Yes. How much is this camera, please?
Woman: Let me see. It's Japanese! Are you from Japan?
Rie: Yes, that's right.
Woman: Well, welcome to America!
Rie: Oh, thank you. And, the camera?
Woman: Oh, yes! This one is three hundred fifty dollars. It's a good deal!
Rie: Ah, OK. I'll take it. Is cash OK?
Woman: Is cash OK? Sure! Cash is just fine!
Rie: OK. Here you are … Three hundred fifty dollars.

Conversation 3: Koji is asking about a motorcycle.

Man: G'day. Can I help you, sir?
Koji: Er, maybe. I want to buy a motorcycle.
Man: Oh! Do you see one that you like?
Koji: Yes, I like this one.
Man: Mm. It's Italian. It's a real beauty!
Koji: How much is it?
Man: Well, twenty thousand dollars.
Koji: What! Er, maybe I'll come back tomorrow!

Conversation 4: Mayumi and Makoto are asking about a dress.

Woman: May I help you, madam?
Mayumi: Er, yes. This dress. How much is it?
Woman: Let's see. That one is … one thousand and, er, sixty-five pounds.
Makoto: How much?!
Woman: One thousand and sixty-five. It's a Ralph Lauren dress, sir.
Mayumi: It's beautiful!
Makoto: It's expensive!

Woman:	Would you like to try it on, madam?
Makoto:	Er, well ...
Mayumi:	Yes, please!
Makoto:	I guess so.

Conversation 5: Miki wants to change some money.

Clerk:	Next, please.
Miki:	Yes, I'd like to change some money, please.
Clerk:	Yes. What would you like to change?
Miki:	Fifteen thousand yen into dollars.
Clerk:	OK. Fifteen thousand yen into U.S. dollars.
Miki:	Yes, please.

Conversation

Listen to this conversation between Rie and a bank clerk. Fill in the blanks.

Rie:	Can I change some money here?
Clerk:	Sure. What would you like to change?
Rie:	I'd like to change twenty thousand yen into dollars, please.
Clerk:	No problem.
Rie:	What's the exchange rate today?
Clerk:	A hundred yen to the dollar.
Rie:	I see. And how much commission do you charge?
Clerk:	Two percent, ma'am.
Rie:	OK.
Clerk:	That comes to one hundred ninety-six dollars.

Unit 4 Do you have any vacancies?

Listening

These people are talking about hotel rooms. Listen. Circle T (true) or F (false).

Conversation 1: Miki and Rie

Clerk:	Hello. How may I help you?
Miki:	Hi! We have a reservation ...
Clerk:	What's your name, please?
Miki:	Miki Kobayashi.
Clerk:	Ah, yes. Miss Kobayashi and Miss Yasuda.
Rie:	We would like one room with two beds, please.
Clerk:	A double room? That's right. You're in room two one four.
Rie:	Good.
Miki:	Yes, that's good!

Conversation 2: Miki and Rie

Miki:	So, how much is that, please?
Clerk:	It's three hundred dollars per night plus tax.
Rie:	Is that three hundred dollars each?
Clerk:	No, that's the room rate. Three hundred total. The price is the same for one or two people in the room.
Miki:	That's fine.

Conversation 3: Joanne Miller

Clerk:	Hello, London Palace Hotel. Can I help you?
Ms. Miller:	Hello. Do you have a double room for three nights?
Clerk:	For three nights? Er, when do you want it?

Ms. Miller:	Well, we'll arrive on Tuesday.
Clerk:	So, three nights from Tuesday?
Ms. Miller:	Er, just let me check with my husband. Sorry.
Clerk:	No problem, madam.
Ms. Miller:	Er, sorry. No, only two nights. Tuesday and Wednesday. Not Thursday.
Clerk:	OK, madam. And the name?
Ms. Miller:	Miller. Joanne Miller.

Conversation 4: Joanne Miller

Clerk:	And may I have a phone number, please? In case we need to get in touch with you.
Ms. Miller:	Er, yes. The number is ... zero one three one ...
Clerk:	Zero one three one, yes.
Ms. Miller:	Four two eight ...
Clerk:	Four two eight.
Ms. Miller:	Seven eight seven seven.
Clerk:	Seven seven eight seven.
Ms. Miller:	Er, no. Seven eight seven seven.
Clerk:	Seven eight double seven. Sorry, madam. Thank you for calling, and we look forward to seeing you next Tuesday.

Conversation 5: Mr. Rosentreter

Clerk:	Good morning. Harbour Hotel.
Mr. Rosentreter:	Er, hello. My name is Rosentreter, Max Rosentreter. I'm calling about a room.
Clerk:	For tonight?
Mr. Rosentreter:	Yes, tonight.
Clerk:	We only have singles left.
Mr. Rosentreter:	That's OK. Er, how much are they, please?
Clerk:	Ninety dollars per night. Australian dollars, that is!
Mr. Rosentreter:	How much? Nineteen? ... One nine?
Clerk:	No, ninety! Nine zero, sir! You won't get a room for nineteen ... no way!
Mr. Rosentreter:	OK, well, of course. Ninety is fine.

Conversation 6: Mr. Rosentreter

Clerk:	What time do you think you'll be here?
Mr. Rosentreter:	Well, my bus arrives at a quarter to six.
Clerk:	A quarter to six? Well, we're only about fifteen minutes away from the bus station.
Mr. Rosentreter:	Fifteen? OK. I'll see you then. At, er, about six.
Clerk:	Fine. See you later, Mr. Rosentreter.

Conversation

Listen to this conversation between Mayumi and a clerk in an Oxford hotel. Fill in the blanks.

Clerk:	Good morning, Garden Hotel. Can I help you?
Mayumi:	Yes, please. Do you have any vacancies for Thursday, please?
Clerk:	Yes, we do. Would you like a single or a double?
Mayumi:	A double, please.
Clerk:	And for how many nights?
Mayumi:	For two nights, please.
Clerk:	Fine.
Mayumi:	How much is it?
Clerk:	It's seventy-six pounds per night.
Mayumi:	That's fine.

Clerk:	OK. Could I have your name, please?
Mayumi:	Yes, it's Kinoshita.
Clerk:	Could you spell that, please?
Mayumi:	Yes, it's K-I-N-O-S-H-I-T-A.
Clerk:	Thank you. And could I have your phone number, please?
Mayumi:	Oh, yes, sure. It's zero one eight one, three four two, nine seven nine nine.

Unit 5 Go straight along Seventh Avenue

Some tourists are in the Hotel Gorham on West Fifty-fifth Street. Where does each person want to go? Listen. Circle each place on the map, then write the name below.

Conversation 1

Tourist:	Excuse me? Is (*beep*) close to here, please?
Man:	Yes, sir. To get there, you go out of here and make a left.
Tourist:	Out of here, then left. Yes.
Man:	Then turn right onto Seventh Avenue.
Tourist:	OK. Right onto Seventh Avenue.
Man:	Yeah, go past the Hotel Wellington.
Tourist:	I understand. Past the Hotel Wellington.
Man:	And you'll see it on the right. You can't miss it. It's on Seventh Avenue between West Fifty-sixth and Fifty-seventh Street.
Tourist:	OK. Thank you very much.
Man:	No problem.

Conversation 2

Tourist:	Can you help me, please?
Man:	Sure! At least, I'll try!
Tourist:	How do I get to (*beep*), please?
Man:	OK. Go out of here and turn left. Then go straight ahead.
Tourist:	OK. Left out of here, then straight ahead.
Man:	Yeah. Go to Broadway, then turn right.
Tourist:	So, Broadway, then turn right.
Man:	Yeah, that's it. Then, go up Broadway one … two … three blocks and you'll see it on your left … on the corner of Broadway and West Fifty-seventh Street.
Tourist:	On the corner of Broadway and West Fifty-seventh. Thank you very much!
Man:	You're welcome! Have a nice day!

Conversation 3

Tourist:	Can you help me? Do you know where the (*beep*) is, please?
Clerk:	Oh, yes. It's quite easy!
Tourist:	I hope so!
Clerk:	Go out of here and turn left.
Tourist:	Left along West Fifty-fifth Street?
Clerk:	Yes, along West Fifty-fifth Street. Then turn right onto Seventh Avenue.
Tourist:	Right onto Seventh Avenue. OK.
Clerk:	After two blocks, you turn right onto West Fifty-seventh Street.
Tourist:	I see. West Fifty-seventh Street.

Clerk:	Yes. Then you'll see it on your right, across from the Pizza Hut.
Tourist:	Thank you.
Clerk:	That's OK.

Conversation 4

Tourist:	Excuse me? Can you tell me where the nearest (*beep*) is?
Man:	Yes. Are you walking?
Tourist:	Yes.
Man:	Well, you want to go out of here and go right.
Tourist:	Up this street?
Man:	Yeah, right on this street, then take the first left.
Tourist:	You mean left on Fifth Avenue?
Man:	No. The next street's Sixth Avenue. Left on Sixth Avenue. OK?
Tourist:	OK.
Man:	OK. Then go up three blocks and you'll see it on the right … near the corner of West Fifty-seventh Street.
Tourist:	The corner of West Fifty-seventh Street.
Man:	You got it!
Tourist:	Thank you.
Man:	Have a nice meal!

Conversation

Rie is in the Hotel Gorham. Listen to this conversation between Rie and the hotel clerk. Fill in the blanks.

Rie:	Excuse me? Do you know where the Manhattan Ocean Club is, please?
Clerk:	Sure. Go out of here, then turn right.
Rie:	Yes, OK.
Clerk:	Then go straight along Sixth Avenue.
Rie:	I see.
Clerk:	Then take the third right.
Rie:	OK.
Clerk:	The club is on your left.
Rie:	Great! Thanks very much for your help.

Unit 6 Do you mind if I watch TV?

Listening

What is Koji asking about? Listen. Check the correct answer.

Conversation 1

Mrs. Todd:	How was your meal, Koji?
Koji:	Sorry?
Mrs. Todd:	Your food! How was it?
Koji:	Oh, it was great. Thanks for letting me use the microwave.
Mrs. Todd:	No problem.
Koji:	Er, er, Mrs. Todd …?
Mrs. Todd:	Yes? Is anything wrong, Koji?
Koji:	Er, well, I have some clothes to wash. Can you show me how to use the washing machine?
Mrs. Todd:	Oh, sure! I'll show you.

Conversation 2

Mr. Todd:	Good morning, Koji! Sleep well? Here, have some coffee!

Koji: Thanks. Er, I was …

Mr. Todd: Is there something wrong with the coffee? Would you prefer tea?

Koji: Oh, no. It's fine, thank you. It's just that I was a little cold last night. Could I have an extra … er, I can't remember the name …

Mr. Todd: Blanket?

Koji: Yes! Could I have an extra blanket tonight, please?

Mr. Todd: Of course. No problem.

Conversation 3

Mrs. Todd: (shouts) That's a great Walkman you've got there, Koji.

Koji: (switches off Walkman) Sorry? I couldn't hear you.

Mrs. Todd: I said, that's a nice Walkman.

Koji: Oh, yes, thank you. I was listening to music.

Mrs. Todd: Well that's OK. But you should practice your English, you know!

Koji: Yes, I know. Er, Mrs. Todd …?

Mrs. Todd: Yes, Koji?

Koji: Is it OK if I watch TV now?

Mrs. Todd: Of course. But it's only the news on, I think.

Koji: But it's good for my English.

Mrs. Todd: Right. Listening to Japanese music won't help your English, that's for sure.

Conversation 4

Mrs. Todd: Sam! Leave Koji alone! Sam! Now, stop that!

Koji: Er, excuse me, Mrs. Todd? When's the best time to take a shower?

Mrs. Todd: Oh, any time, really. But the best time is the evening. The bathroom gets pretty busy in the morning.

Koji: OK. So, evenings are best. (pause) Er, Mrs. Todd, could I take Sam for a walk?

Mrs. Todd: Oh, sure. Go ahead.

Koji: Great! Come on, Sam!

Conversation 5

Koji: Mr. Todd, do you mind if two of my friends visit tomorrow evening?

Mr. Todd: No, that's fine. You can take them to your room.

Koji: Thank you. Er, I wanted to ask you …

Mr. Todd: Ah. Go ahead.

Koji: Well, both of my friends smoke. Do you mind if they smoke in my room?

Mr. Todd: Well, we don't really like smoking, Koji. It's the smell.

Koji: That's OK. I'll just tell them not to smoke in the house.

Mr. Todd: Thank you, Koji.

Conversation 6

Koji: Mrs. Todd …?

Mrs. Todd: Yes?

Koji: Sorry to interrupt you.

Mrs. Todd: That's all right. The show's over.

Koji: Could I call Japan, please? I'll make a collect call.

Mrs. Todd: Of course, Koji. But would you mind waiting for

half an hour? My favorite TV show is about to start!

Koji: Oh, yes. Sure. Thanks.

Announcer: And now … this break for these messages.

Conversation

Listen to this conversation between Koji and Mrs. Todd. Fill in the blanks.

Mrs. Todd: Here are your front door keys, Koji.

Koji: Thanks, Mrs. Todd.

Mrs. Todd: Now, is there anything else you want to ask?

Koji: Yes, please. Do you mind if I take a bath?

Mrs. Todd: Of course not. I'll give you a towel.

Koji: And could you show me how to use the shower?

Mrs. Todd: Oh, it's easy. I'll show you now.

Koji: Thank you very much. Oh, yes … and is it OK if I go out this evening?

Mrs. Todd: Yes, that's fine. But please don't be late home.

Koji: OK. Thanks.

Unit 7 How do you feel?

Listening

What is wrong with each person? Listen. Check the correct answer.

Conversation 1: Koji

Doctor: Good morning.

Koji: (hoarse) I'm sorry. I can't speak.

Doctor: Oh! You're having problems with your throat!

Koji: Yes! I can't speak.

Doctor: Mm. Now, can you open wide … Wide, please.

Koji: Er, like this? (spoken with difficulty)

Doctor: That's it, nice and wide. Ah yes, it looks quite sore.

Koji: Can I close it now? (spoken incomprehensibly)

Doctor: What was that?

Koji: I said, can I close it now?

Doctor: Just a moment. Can you say "Aaah?"

Koji: Aaah. Oh, it's horrible! It hurts.

Conversation 2: Rie

Doctor: Good morning.

Rie: Good morning.

Doctor: What can I do for you?

Rie: I have an earache in both ears.

Doctor: Both ears?

Rie: Yes, they both hurt.

Doctor: When did the pain start?

Rie: About two days ago.

Doctor: I see. Let me take a look, then. Now, just sit still …

Conversation 3: Miki

Doctor: Good afternoon. Are you Miss, em, Ko... Koba...

Miki: Kobayashi, yes.

Doctor: Yes, thanks. And what seems to be the problem?

Miki: I went shopping yesterday and I bought a lot of things. I think it was all too heavy for me!

Doctor:	So, you have a sore back?
Miki:	Yes.
Doctor:	Where does it hurt?
Miki:	Just here.
Doctor:	Here.
Miki:	Itaii! (*Japanese expression of pain*) Yes!

Conversation 4: Makoto

Doctor:	Hello. Makoto Kinoshita, right?
Makoto:	Yes.
Doctor:	Well, what can I do for you?
Makoto:	Um, I have a pain, here.
Doctor:	In your stomach?
Makoto:	Yes. You see, I had some English food last night.
Doctor:	English food? Oh, I see. You aren't used to English food.
Makoto:	No, I prefer Japanese food.
Doctor:	Well, I don't think it's serious. This often happens when you're on holiday. Do you have a headache?
Makoto:	No, just here, my stomach.
Doctor:	Well, don't worry about it. I'll give you something to make you feel better.

Conversation

Listen and check your answers.

Doctor:	Good morning. Could I have your name, please?
Mayumi:	I'm Mayumi Kinoshita.
Doctor:	What can I do for you?
Mayumi:	I have a stomachache.
Doctor:	Mm. When did it start hurting?
Mayumi:	Yesterday.
Doctor:	I see. How do you feel now?
Mayumi:	Terrible. It's very painful.
Doctor:	Right. I'll give you a prescription for something to help you. Take it three times a day before meals.
Mayumi:	Thank you, doctor.

Unit 8 Are you free this weekend?

Listening

When will these people meet? Listen. Write the day and time.

Conversation 1: Miki

Amy:	Hello.
Miki:	Hello. Is this Amy Blake?
Amy:	Yes, this is Amy Blake speaking.
Miki:	Hi! It's Miki here, from Japan.
Amy:	Hello there! I thought I recognized your voice. How are you? And where are you?
Miki:	I'm fine. I'm here in New York, at the Hotel Gorham.
Amy:	That's great!
Miki:	I was wondering. Are you free on Wednesday evening?
Amy:	Wednesday? Sure.
Miki:	Would you like to come to dinner? I'm here with my friend, Rie.

Amy:	Dinner together? That sounds like a great idea.
Miki:	Well, how about meeting here at the Gorham, at seven thirty?
Amy:	The Gorham on Wednesday at seven thirty. Well, that's fine. I can't wait to see you again.
Miki:	OK. See you on Wednesday, then.
Amy:	Bye!
Miki:	Bye!

Conversation 2: Mayumi

Mayumi:	Hello?
Yvette:	Oh, Mayumi. Hi!
Mayumi:	Er, hello. Who's this, please?
Yvette:	It's me, Yvette. We met in Paris last week.
Mayumi:	Oh, hello! Are you in London?
Yvette:	Yes. I had to come here on business.
Mayumi:	What a nice surprise! We must get together.
Yvette:	Well, I want to invite you to the theater.
Mayumi:	That's very kind. I hope I can understand it!
Yvette:	Me, too! How about Thursday?
Mayumi:	Oh! I'm sorry. I can't make it then. Would Friday be OK?
Yvette:	No problem. Let's meet at six o'clock at the National Theatre.
Mayumi:	Six?
Yvette:	Yes, then we can eat something first.
Mayumi:	OK. Great. See you on Friday, then.

Conversation 3: Koji

Pete:	Koji? Koji!
Koji:	Oh! Hi, Pete.
Pete:	Hi! What are you doing here?
Koji:	Oh, I'm just doing some shopping.
Pete:	Listen. We must get together some time.
Koji:	Yeah, that would be fun.
Pete:	OK. Well, let's think. What are you doing this weekend?
Koji:	This weekend? Well, I'm going to the movies on Sunday afternoon …
Pete:	What about Saturday?
Koji:	I don't have any plans.
Pete:	Good. Well, why don't you come over. I just bought a new motorcycle – a Honda CBR nine hundred Fireblade. You can try it out!
Koji:	Really? I can try it?
Pete:	Sure you can. Can you come over at ten o'clock?
Koji:	Ten o'clock on Saturday? Great!
Pete:	OK, see you then.
Koji:	I'll be there! Bye!

Conversation

Listen to this conversation between Makoto and his friend, John Taylor. Fill in the blanks.

John:	Hi, Makoto. It's John here.
Makoto:	Oh, hello, John.
John:	I was just wondering. Would you like to meet for lunch today?
Makoto:	That sounds great! Oh, wait! I'm sorry. I'm afraid I'm busy then, but how about Thursday?
John:	Yes, I think I can make that.
Makoto:	What time should we meet?

John:	How about twelve thirty?
Makoto:	Fine! Should we meet here, at my hotel?
John:	OK, great! See you then!
Makoto:	Yes, see you, and thanks for inviting me!

Unit 9 Are you ready to order?

Listening

These people are ordering food in restaurants. Listen. Match each conversation with the correct food order.

Conversation 1: Miki and Rie

Server:	Would you like to see the menu?
Miki:	No, thank you. I think we know what we want.
Server:	Fine. Would you like an appetizer?
Rie:	Not for me.
Miki:	No, thanks.
Server:	OK. What would you like as an entrée?
Miki:	I'd like the seafood pizza, please.
Rie:	And I'll have the pepperoni pizza.
Server:	Would you like a salad with that?
Miki:	No, thanks.
Rie:	I don't think so.
Server:	And to drink?
Miki:	A glass of orange juice, please.
Rie:	And a glass of red wine, please.
Server:	All right. Would you like anything else?
Miki:	No. That's all, thank you.
Server:	OK.

Conversation 2: Makoto and Mayumi

Server:	Are you ready to order?
Makoto:	Yes, I think so.
Mayumi:	Er, yes.
Server:	What would you like?
Makoto:	Er, I'd like the seafood pasta, please.
Server:	Yes.
Mayumi:	Um, what's fettucine bolognese?
Server:	It's pasta with meat sauce.
Mayumi:	Fine. I'll have that.
Server:	And what would you like to drink?
Makoto:	A glass of white wine, please.
Mayumi:	And a glass of red wine for me.
Server:	Certainly, madam.

Conversation 3: Koji and Pete

Pete:	Can we order now?
Server:	Sure. What can I get you?
Pete:	A beer and an orange juice, please.
Server:	You just want drinks. No food?
Pete:	No, we want food, too.
Server:	Ah, OK.
Pete:	Ah, I guess I'll have the steak.
Server:	How would you like that?
Pete:	Medium, please.
Server:	And for you?
Koji:	The chicken salad, please.
Pete:	And could you bring the check with the food, please? I'm afraid we're in a hurry.
Server:	OK. Your order won't be long.

Conversation

Listen and check your answers.

Server:	What would you like for dessert?
Miki:	I'm not sure. What's Black Forest Gateau?
Server:	It's chocolate cake.
Miki:	That sounds interesting. I think I'll try that.
Server:	Would you like coffee?
Miki:	Mm, yes. I'd like an espresso, please.
Server:	Fine.
Miki:	Oh, and may we have the check, please?
Server:	Certainly. Your order won't be long.

Unit 10 My father works in a bank

Listening

Miki is talking about her family to her friend, Amy. Listen. Circle T (true) or F (false).

Conversation 1

Miki:	This is my father.
Amy:	And is that your mom?
Miki:	Yes. She's a travel agent.
Amy:	And what does your father do?
Miki:	He works in a bank.
Amy:	Which bank?
Miki:	The Sumitomo Bank.

Conversation 2

Amy:	And what about you?
Miki:	Me?
Amy:	Do you want to work in a travel agency, like your mom?
Miki:	Well, she wants me to.
Amy:	But what do you think?
Miki:	Em, I haven't decided yet. But no, I don't really want to work in a travel agency.

Conversation 3

Amy:	And I see in this photo that you've got one brother and one sister, right?
Miki:	Er, no. I don't have a brother. That's my cousin. But this is my sister.
Amy:	And how old is she?
Miki:	Kimiko's fourteen.
Amy:	Oh! She's quite a bit younger than you.
Miki:	Yes. But she wanted to come to America with me!

Conversation 4

Amy:	And this is your house? You live in Tokyo?
Miki:	Not really in Tokyo. It's a suburb, north of Tokyo.
Amy:	And does your father drive to work from there?
Miki:	Oh, no! There's too much traffic. We take the train. Our house is about fifteen minutes from the station.
Amy:	So you walk to the station and get a train from there into the city?
Miki:	Right.

Conversation 5

Amy:	And what do you do on weekends, Miki? Do you have any hobbies?
Miki:	Well, I sometimes play tennis with my friends. And I usually go shopping on Sundays.
Amy:	On Sundays? Are all the stores open on Sundays in Japan.
Miki:	Oh, yes. And I love to go shopping then.
Amy:	Born to shop, huh, Miki?
Miki:	(*laughs*)

Conversation

Listen to this conversation between Rie and Amy. Fill in the blanks.

Amy:	Tell me about your family, Rie.
Rie:	I have a photo of them. Would you like to see it?
Amy:	Yes, please.
Rie:	Well, this is my father. He's forty-two years old.
Amy:	What does he do?
Rie:	He works for Sony.
Amy:	Oh, really? And your mother?
Rie:	She's a schoolteacher.
Amy:	Do you have any brothers and sisters?
Rie:	Yes, I have one brother and one sister.
Amy:	I see. Tell me, where do you live?
Rie:	Well, we live in a small apartment in the suburbs of Tokyo.
Amy:	I see. So, what do you usually do on weekends?
Rie:	I like to play tennis.
Amy:	Wow! I didn't know you could do that!

Unit 11 What's your favorite food?

Listening

Here are some ideas that the Todds have about Japan. Koji and the Todds are talking about them. Does Koji agree? Listen. Circle Y (Yes) or N (No).

Conversation 1

Mrs. Todd:	Are you writing home, Koji?
Koji:	Yes! This is the first time. I've been so busy!
Mrs. Todd:	Gosh! Japanese looks so different! It's like Chinese, isn't it?
Koji:	Not really. In fact, Japanese and Chinese are very different.
Mrs. Todd:	Really? They look the same.
Koji:	Well, we use some Chinese characters, called "kanji", but the characters usually have a different pronunciation.
Mrs. Todd:	Oh, I see.
Koji:	And Japanese also uses two other writing systems, "hiragana" and "katakana".
Mrs. Todd:	What? Two? Why?
Koji:	Well, we use "hiragana" for writing Japanese words and "katakana" for writing foreign words.
Mrs. Todd:	Gosh! You must be very clever, Koji!
Koji:	No, I'm not so clever. I'm just Japanese!

Conversation 2

Mr. Todd:	Koji, how big is Japan?
Koji:	Mm. Japan is about the same size as California.
Mr. Todd:	Really. So small?
Koji:	Yes. And … about eighty per cent of Japan is almost empty. Most people in Japan live in a few big cities.
Mr. Todd:	So, what is the population of Japan?
Koji:	About a hundred twenty-three million.
Mr. Todd:	Wow!
Koji:	Yeah, and most people live in a few big cities.
Mr. Todd:	Incredible! So the cities are very crowded.
Koji:	Yeah. They're definitely crowded.

Conversation 3

Mrs. Todd:	What about pollution, Koji. Isn't the air in Tokyo very dirty?
Koji:	Well, it was bad, I think, but it's not so bad now.
Mrs. Todd:	But I saw a picture of people in Tokyo wearing white masks over their faces.
Koji:	Yes, some people do wear masks, but not because of pollution. It's because they have a cold and they don't want other people to catch it!
Mrs. Todd:	Ah, I see! There's so many things we don't know about Japan.
Koji:	Well, there are many things I don't know about Australia!

Conversation 4

Mrs. Todd:	How do you like Australian food, Koji?
Koji:	It's nice. I like it.
Mrs. Todd:	It must be different after raw fish and rice.
Koji:	Actually, we don't eat raw fish every day. There are many different kinds of Japanese food.
Mrs. Todd:	Oh, yeah?
Koji:	Yes. If you like, I'll cook Japanese food for you one day.
Mrs. Todd:	Really? That would be great. But … er, would we have to eat raw fish?
Koji:	Only if you want to.

Conversation

Listen and check your answers.

Mrs. Todd:	Is Japanese food the same as Chinese food?
Koji:	Not really. In fact, it's quite different.
Mrs. Todd:	Oh, I see. What's your favorite food?
Koji:	I like "tempura" best.
Mrs. Todd:	What's that?
Koji:	It's deep-fried seafood and vegetables.

Unit 12 What would you like to drink?

Listening

Koji and Pete are in a pub in Sydney. Listen. Circle T (true) or F (false).

Conversation 1

Pete:	What would you like to drink, Koji?
Koji:	Oh, thanks, Pete. A beer, please.

Pete:	Two schooners, please.
Bartender:	OK, mate.
Pete:	So, Koji, are you enjoying Sydney?
Koji:	Yes, I'm having a great time.
Pete:	Good.
Bartender:	There you go. Two schooners. That's four dollars twenty cents, please.
Pete:	OK. Thanks.
Pete:	Cheers, Koji!
Koji:	Cheers, Pete! (*drinks*) Mm.
Pete:	(*drinks*) Ahh. And what do you think of Australian beer, Koji?
Koji:	Mm. I love it. I like it better than Japanese beer.
Pete:	Good on ya', mate.

Conversation 2

Koji:	It's my round, Pete. Same again?
Pete:	Yes, thanks.
Koji:	Two more schooners, please.
Bartender:	OK, mate.
Pete:	Tell me, Koji, have you tried 'gator meat yet?
Koji:	Sorry? 'Gator meat? I don't understand.
Pete:	Alligator meat. Have you tried alligator meat yet?
Koji:	Ugh! Alligator? No. You must be joking!
Pete:	Oh, you have to try it, Koji. I think you'd like it.
Koji:	I don't think so, Pete. But maybe we should eat something. How about a pizza?
Pete:	Sure. I know a good pizza place.
Bartender:	There you go. Two schooners. Four twenty, please.
Pete:	But first we have to finish these. Cheers!
Koji:	Cheers!

Miki and Rie are at their friend Amy's house. Listen. Circle T (true) or F (false).

Conversation 3

Amy:	(*doorbell rings*) Hey! Miki! Rie! Glad you could make it.
Miki:	Well, thank you for inviting us! These are for you.
Amy:	Flowers! Why, thank you. They're beautiful. You really shouldn't have. Come and meet my friends. ... Carol, this is Miki, and this is Rie.
Miki:	Nice to meet you.
Rie:	Nice to meet you.
Carol:	Well, it's great to meet you, too. Are you having a good time here?
Miki:	Yes, we're having a great time. Everyone is so friendly.

Conversation 4

Party-goer:	So, Miki and Rie, how long have you been here?
Miki:	About ...
Rie:	... ten days?
Miki:	Yes, about ten days.
Party-goer:	And what have you done so far?
Miki:	Mostly sightseeing and shopping.
Party-goer:	Oh, yeah? What have you seen?
Miki:	Well, we went to the Statue of Liberty and the Empire State Building ...

Rie:	And the Museum of Modern Art.
Party-goer:	Great! What did you think of it?
Rie:	It was very interesting. There's so much to see.
Party-goer:	So, are you staying in New York for long?
Rie:	No, we're flying to San Francisco tomorrow. We want to see the Golden Gate Bridge.

Conversation

Listen to this conversation between Makoto and John Taylor. Fill in the blanks.

John:	What would you like to drink, Makoto?
Makoto:	Oh, could I have a pint of lager, please, John?:
John:	Sure. So, are you enjoying London?
Makoto:	Yes, I'm having a great time!
John:	Good! Have you been to Oxford Street yet?
Makoto:	Yes, I have. It was very busy.
John:	And what do you think of British food?
Makoto:	Well, it's different!

Unit 13   I won't be home for lunch today

Listening

What is each person planning to do? Listen. Check the correct answer.

Conversation 1: Koji and Mrs. Todd

Mrs. Todd:	Are you going out, Koji? Bye! See you at lunch.
Koji:	I'm sorry, Mrs. Todd, but I won't be back for lunch today.
Mrs. Todd:	Oh, well that's all right. What are your plans for today, then? The beach?
Koji:	Er, no. I'm meeting my friends at the swimming pool. We're going for a swim.
Mrs. Todd:	But you could go to the beach. It's such a lovely day.
Koji:	Mm. I don't really like swimming in the ocean.
Mrs. Todd:	Oh, OK. Well, have a great time at the pool.

Conversation 2: Rie and Amy

Amy:	What are you doing tonight, Rie?
Rie:	I'm not sure, Amy. Miki ...
Amy:	Well, we're having a barbecue if you want to come.
Rie:	Miki wants to see a movie, but ...
Amy:	Oh! This weather is too hot for movies!
Rie:	Mm, maybe you're right. OK. I'll come to the barbecue.
Amy:	Great!
Rie:	I'll tell Miki.
Amy:	Sure! See you both later.

Conversation 3: Mayumi and John

Mayumi:	Hello?
John:	Mayumi? Is that you?
Mayumi:	Yes ... John! How are you?
John:	Fine, thanks. Listen, I was wondering if you have any plans for tonight.
Mayumi:	Tonight? Oh, yes. We're going to go ...

John:	You see, we're going out for pizza. Would you like to come?
Mayumi:	Oh, sorry, we can't. We already made plans. We're going to a Japanese restaurant. Makoto wants to eat Japanese food!
John:	Oh, right! Fine. Well, maybe I'll call next week, and we can go out then?
Mayumi:	Yes, that would be fun. Thanks, John. Bye.
John:	Bye.

Conversation 4: Miki and Amy

Amy:	What are your plans for tomorrow, Miki?
Miki:	Oh, I haven't decided yet.
Amy:	Do you want to go shopping with me?
Miki:	Oh, yes! That's a great idea, Amy! … No, wait. Oh, I can't! I've just remembered – I'm going to the zoo!
Amy:	Never mind! We can go shopping another day.

Conversation

Listen and check your answers.

Mr. Todd:	What are your plans for today, Koji?
Koji:	I'm going on a school trip.
Mr. Todd:	Oh, really? Where are you going?
Koji:	To the Australian Wildlife Park. I want to see some typical Aussie animals.
Mr. Todd:	That sounds good. Don't forget your camera.
Koji:	No, I won't. Oh, yes! Sorry, but I won't be home for dinner tonight. I'm going to a barbecue with my friends.
Mr. Todd:	That's OK. Thanks for telling me. When will you be back?
Koji:	I'm not sure exactly, but I should be home around ten thirty.
Mr. Todd:	That's fine. Call if you're going to be late.
Koji:	OK. Bye!

Unit 14 Could you tell me when we're there, please?

Listening

Listen to these conversations about buses. Circle T (true) or F (false).

Conversation 1: New York

Tourist:	Excuse me?
Driver:	Hi! Can I help?
Tourist:	Oh, hello. Which bus goes to Battery Park, please?
Driver:	To Battery Park? You need the six.
Tourist:	The six? Not the sixteen?
Driver:	No, the six. That's the one you need.
Tourist:	Oh, OK. Thank you.
Driver:	You're welcome.

Conversation 2: San Francisco

Rie:	Em, excuse me?
Woman:	You need any help?
Rie:	Oh, yes, thank you. Does the San Francisco city tour leave from here?
Woman:	Sorry? I didn't catch that.
Rie:	Er, the city tour. Does it leave from here?
Woman:	No. You need to go around the corner.
Rie:	Around the corner?
Woman:	Yeah. The stop for the city tour is around the corner.
Rie:	Oh, I see. Thanks.
Woman:	No problem.

Conversation 3: Australia

Woman:	Er, how much is it to Balmain, please?
Driver:	Balmain? Are you going to Balmain?
Woman:	Er, yes. Balmain.
Driver:	But this isn't the Balmain bus.
Woman:	Sorry, I don't understand.
Driver:	This is the four three one. You need the four three three or the four three four.
Woman:	Sorry?
Driver:	You're on the wrong bus. You don't want the four three one.
Woman:	Oh, I see. Thank you very much.

Conversation 4: Australia

Man:	Er, excuse me?
Driver:	Yes?
Man:	Er, when do we get to Macquarie University?
Driver:	To Macquarie University?
Man:	Yes, Macquarie. Could you tell me when to get off?
Driver:	I'm sorry, but you're on the wrong bus.
Man:	The wrong bus? Oh, but this is the four three oh, isn't it?
Driver:	Yes, it is. But this is going to the other university, Sydney University, not Macquarie.
Man:	Oh, no!
Driver:	Don't worry. Everyone makes the same mistake.
Man:	Yes, but I'm going to miss my appointment!

Conversation 5: Britain

Makoto:	Excuse me.
Man:	Yes. Can I help?
Makoto:	Which bus goes to the city centre, please?
Man:	The sixteen.
Makoto:	Ah, thank you. The sixty.
Man:	No, the sixteen. You want the number sixteen.
Makoto:	OK, thank you. Sixty. Sixty. Thank you. Goodbye.
Man:	Oh, no. He'll never get there. The sixty goes to the zoo!

Conversation 6: Britain

Man:	Excuse me? Is this the bus for Victoria Station?
Driver:	That's right.
Man:	Oh, good! How much is it, please?
Driver:	Are you going all the way?
Man:	Sorry?
Woman:	Are you going all the way to Victoria?
Man:	Oh, yes. I want to go to Victoria.
Woman:	OK. That's one pound forty.
Man:	OK. Thank you. Excuse me?

Woman: Yes?
Man: Could you tell me when we're there, please?
Woman: Sorry?
Man: Er, could you tell me when to get off, please?
Woman: It's easy. It's the last stop.
Man: Oh, I see. Thank you.

Conversation

Listen and check your answers.

Koji: Excuse me? What time is the next bus for Manly?
Driver: This is it. It leaves in ten minutes.
Koji: Oh, great! How much is that, please?
Driver: That'll be two dollars and fifty cents.
Koji: OK. Here you are.
Driver: Thank you.
Koji: Er, could you tell me when to get off, please?
Driver: Sorry? What was that?
Koji: Um, could you tell me when we're there, please?
Driver: It's easy. Manly's the last stop.
Koji: Oh, OK. Thank you.

Unit 15 How would you like to pay?

Listening

These people are shopping. Listen. Fill in the blanks.

Conversation 1: Mayumi is buying a scarf.

Mayumi: Um, excuse me.
Clerk: Yes, madam. How may I help you?
Mayumi: I'm looking for a scarf.
Clerk: A scarf? Scarves are over here, madam. Do you have a particular design or color in mind?
Mayumi: Mm … I like this one here. How much is it, please?
Clerk: This green one costs … let me see … fifty-eight pounds.
Mayumi: Oh, OK. I'll take it.
Clerk: Certainly. And how will you be paying, madam?
Mayumi: Excuse me?
Clerk: How will you be paying? Which method of payment? In cash?
Mayumi: Oh, my husband is paying.
Clerk: Sir?
Makoto: Mm. How much is it?
Clerk: Fifty-eight pounds, sir.
Makoto: I see. Credit card, then. Do you accept Visa?
Clerk: Visa? Certainly, sir.

Conversation 2: Koji is buying a shirt.

Clerk: Hi, there. Do you need any help?
Koji: Yes, I'd like a cotton shirt, please.
Clerk: A cotton shirt? Certainly. Any particular color?
Koji: Oh, blue. Blue, please.
Clerk: What size?
Koji: Size? Er, I'm not sure. It's for me, but I don't know about Australian sizes.
Clerk: No problem. You're a medium, I think.
Koji: Medium?
Clerk: Yes. We have this one at fifty-five dollars.

Koji: Fifty-five? Mm.
Clerk: Would you like to try it on?
Koji: No, it's OK thank you. I'll take it.
Clerk: Sure. Are you paying cash?
Koji: Er, do you take American Express?
Clerk: Yes, we do.

Conversation 3: Miki is buying a skirt.

Miki: Excuse me. Where will I find ladies clothes, please?
Clerk: Ladieswear? On this floor, ma'am. Perhaps I can help you?
Miki: I'm looking for a skirt.
Clerk: Skirts? Over here. Which color would you like?
Miki: Black, please.
Clerk: This one is very nice.
Miki: Mm. How much is it?
Clerk: This one's one hundred thirty-two dollars.
Miki: I see. Can I try it on, please?
Clerk: Certainly, madam. The dressing rooms are over there.
Miki: Yes, I'll take it. One hundred thirty-two dollars, did you say?
Clerk: Yes. Will you be paying by credit card?
Miki: No, in cash.
Clerk: Cash? Certainly, madam.

Conversation 4: Makoto is buying some shoes.

Clerk: Hello. Can I help you?
Makoto: Yes. Do you have this shoe in a size eight, please?
Clerk: Let me check for you, sir. Here we are. Size eight.
Makoto: Mm. I think they're a little small.
Clerk: Do you want to try an eight and a half?
Makoto: Ah, OK. Yes, please. Oh, that's better. And these are how much? Eighty-nine pounds?
Clerk: Er, eighty-nine? No, I'm afraid they're ninety-eight pounds, sir.
Makoto: Ah. Do you take traveler's checks?
Clerk: Yes, sir. We do.

Conversation

Listen to this conversation between Mayumi and a salesclerk. Fill in the blanks.

Clerk: May I help you?
Mayumi: Yes, please. I'm looking for a blouse.
Clerk: What size would you like?
Mayumi: Small, please.
Clerk: We have this style.
Mayumi: Mm. Very nice. But do you have something in white?
Clerk: Certainly. Here you are. This one's eighty-five pounds.
Mayumi: Fine. I'll take it.
Clerk: Very good. How would you like to pay?
Mayumi: Do you take American Express?
Clerk: Certainly. Would you like to come this way?

Unit 16 Can I send this airmail?

Listening

What does each person want to do? Listen. Check the correct answer.

Conversation 1: Koji

Clerk:	Next, please.
Customer:	Hey, you. You're next.
Koji:	Oh, sorry.
Clerk:	Yes? Can I help you?
Koji:	Er, I'd like to send this package, please.
Clerk:	Where to, sir?
Koji:	Oh, Japan. To Japan.
Clerk:	I'll need to weigh it.
Koji:	OK.
Clerk:	Thank you sir. Now, let's see …

Conversation 2: Rie

Clerk:	Yes, can I help you?
Rie:	Ah, yes. Thank you. But my English isn't very good.
Clerk:	No problem. What is it you want?
Rie:	Like this, um, for a letter?
Clerk:	Oh, you mean stamps? You want some stamps?
Rie:	No, no, not stamps. Like this. Long, and you write on them.
Clerk:	Oh, I know what you want. Aerograms. These?
Rie:	Oh yes, aerograms, thank you. Six, please.
Clerk:	There you are.

Conversation 3: Makoto

Clerk:	Yes?
Makoto:	I'd like to buy, er, for the telephone. Like money.
Clerk:	The telephone? Er, money?
Makoto:	Yes, like money for the telephone.
Clerk:	A phonecard!
Makoto:	Yes, thank you. It's the same word in Japanese! How much are they, please?
Clerk:	We've got cards at four pounds, ten pounds, and twenty pounds.
Makoto:	Oh, then one at ten pounds, please.

Conversation 4: Miki

Clerk:	Next, please.
Miki:	Hello. I'd like to buy some stamps, please.
Clerk:	For those?
Miki:	Yes, for these postcards.
Clerk:	Where are they going? To Japan?
Miki:	No, to my friends in Italy and France.
Clerk:	OK.
Miki:	How much is that, please?
Clerk:	Ah, let's see. That'll be three dollars and twenty cents.
Miki:	OK. Here you are.
Clerk:	Thank you.

Conversation 5: Koji

Clerk:	Hello. Beautiful day, isn't it?
Koji:	Er, sorry?
Clerk:	I said, it's a beautiful day.
Koji:	Oh, yes. Yes.
Clerk:	Now, how can I help you?
Koji:	Er, a registered letter, please.
Clerk:	Yes, where to?
Koji:	Er, er, to me.
Clerk:	Sorry? To you?
Koji:	Yes, er, me.
Clerk:	Sorry, you want to send a registered letter to yourself?
Koji:	Er, no. Sorry. Look. I have this.
Clerk:	Er, let's see. Oh, right. You're here to pick up a registered letter.
Koji:	Yes. It arrived yesterday, but I was out.
Clerk:	OK. Just a minute, please. I'll need to check.

Conversation

Listen to this conversation between Mayumi and a post office clerk. Fill in the blanks.

Clerk:	Next, please.
Mayumi:	Hello. I'd like to buy twelve stamps for these postcards, please.
Clerk:	Sure. Where to?
Mayumi:	Japan.
Clerk:	OK. Let's see. That's four pounds twenty, please.
Mayumi:	Thank you. Oh, and what's the cheapest way to send this package to Japan?
Clerk:	By surface mail.
Mayumi:	I see. And how long will that take?
Clerk:	It'll take about twelve weeks.
Mayumi:	OK, fine.

Unit 17 What time does the show start?

Listening

These people are at the theater. Listen. Circle T (true) or F (false).

Conversation 1: Miki

Clerk:	Can I help you?
Miki:	Yes. I'd like two tickets for Sunset Boulevard, please.
Clerk:	Is that for tonight?
Miki:	Yes, please.
Clerk:	Well, the only ones I have for tonight are seats in the orchestra.
Miki:	Oh, that's good.
Clerk:	They're, let me see … one hundred dollars each.
Miki:	Excuse me? One hundred each?
Clerk:	Yes, that's right. It's a very popular show.
Miki:	Oh, um, but, that's too expensive.
Clerk:	Well, I'm sorry. I can't help you, then.
Miki:	OK. Thanks anyway. One hundred dollars!

Conversation 2: Makoto

Clerk:	Hello, Shaftesbury Lane Theatre.
Makoto:	Hello. Do you have two tickets for Wednesday?
Clerk:	Wednesday? One moment, sir. Ah, no, I'm sorry. We don't have anything at all for Wednesday.
Makoto:	Ah, I see.

Clerk:	Would you like to try Thursday?
Makoto:	Oh, well, OK. Thanks.
Clerk:	Let's see. Thursday. Well, we haven't any stalls, but I can do two in the dress circle.
Makoto:	Dress circle? OK, I'll take those.
Clerk:	Fine. They're thirty pounds each. Could I have your credit card details, please?
Makoto:	Yes. The name is Kinoshita, Makoto Kinoshita.

Conversation 3: Koji

Koji:	(*under his breath*) Row E … row D … row C … Eeee? (*Japanese expression of surprise*)
Usher:	Er, hello. Is there a problem? Can I help?
Koji:	Oh, yes. Thank you. Someone is sitting in my seat. C5.
Usher:	May I see your ticket.
Koji:	Here. C5.
Usher:	Oh yes, but this ticket is for the dress circle.
Koji:	Sorry?
Usher:	Your seat number is C5. But this is the stalls. Your ticket's for the dress circle.
Koji:	Dress what?
Usher:	The dress circle. Upstairs.
Koji:	Ah. My seat's upstairs.
Usher:	Yes, sir. The dress circle. The stairs are over there.
Koji:	Thank you.

Conversation 4: Mayumi

John:	Well, Mayumi. What did you think?
Mayumi:	Er, well, sorry. (*sniff*)
John:	Mayumi, what's wrong? Is anything wrong?
Mayumi:	Oh, I'm sorry, John. (*sniff*)
John:	What's the matter? Don't you feel well? Are you OK?
Mayumi:	No, no. It isn't that. It was the movie.
John:	You didn't like it? I thought you loved "Roman Holiday."
Mayumi:	Er, no! Yes, yes, I do like it.
John:	You do like it? Then why are you crying, Mayumi?
Mayumi:	It was so beautiful, and so sad. (*sniff*) I loved it!
Makoto:	My wife is very romantic, John.

Conversation

Listen and check your answers.

Miki:	Do you have two tickets for "Cats"?
Clerk:	When would you like to go?
Miki:	I'd like to go tomorrow, please.
Clerk:	And is that for the matinée or the evening performance?
Miki:	Oh, the evening, if possible.
Clerk:	Hm. I'm afraid that performance is sold out.
Miki:	How about Tuesday evening?
Clerk:	Er, yes. I have seats in the mezzanine.
Miki:	Mm. What else do you have?
Clerk:	Hm. I have two rear orchestra.
Miki:	How much are they?
Clerk:	They're sixty-seven dollars each.
Miki:	Fine. I'll take them.

Unit 18 Where did you lose it?

Listening

What has each person lost? Listen. Check the correct answer.

Conversation 1: Mayumi

Clerk:	Next, please.
Mayumi:	Can you help me? I think I left something on a train.
Clerk:	Yes, and which train was that?
Mayumi:	From Brighton to London.
Clerk:	From Brighton. Yes, and which train? What time was it?
Mayumi:	It left Brighton at nine o'clock this morning.
Clerk:	OK, the oh nine hundred train. What kind of bag is it?
Mayumi:	Um…
Clerk:	Is it a large bag?
Mayumi:	Oh, no. It's quite small.
Clerk:	And what's it made of?
Mayumi:	It's made of leather.
Clerk:	And the color? What color is it?
Mayumi:	Um, black, I think. Oh, wait. No, I think it's blue.
Clerk:	OK. Blue. I'll just check.
Mayumi:	Thank you.

Conversation 2: Miki

Miki:	Excuse me?
Clerk:	Yes. May I help you?
Miki:	Yes. I was here at the theater last night.
Clerk:	Yes?
Miki:	Well, I think I left my umbrella.
Clerk:	I see. And where did you leave it?
Miki:	Close to my seat.
Clerk:	OK, but where were you sitting?
Miki:	In the orchestra, Row M. In the middle of the row.
Clerk:	Right. What color is it?
Miki:	Oh, it's blue and white.
Clerk:	Just a minute. I'll check. (*shouted aside*) Frank! Did anyone find a blue and white umbrella in the orchestra?
Frank:	(*shouted aside*) Er, no, I don't think so! But we found a yellow one.
Clerk:	We found a yellow one, but not a blue and white one.
Miki:	No? Oh, well.
Clerk:	I'm sorry, lady. I think someone took it.
Miki:	Never mind. Thanks anyway.

Conversation 3: Koji

Clerk:	Yes. Next. What's the problem, sir?
Koji:	I lost something here yesterday.
Clerk:	You lost something?
Koji:	Yes, I think it was near the kangaroos.
Clerk:	Well, what was it?
Koji:	A shopping bag.
Clerk:	Just a shopping bag? Is that all?
Koji:	Er, no. It had a camera in it.
Clerk:	I see. Can you describe the bag?

Koji:	It was a shopping bag from a department store.
Clerk:	Which department store?
Koji:	David Jones.
Clerk:	David Jones. Just a minute, I'll look for it.
Koji:	Thank you.
Clerk:	(*coming back*) You're very lucky. It's here! And the camera's still inside!
Koji:	Oh, that's great. Thank you very much.

Conversation 4: Makoto

Clerk:	Hello, Reception. How may I help you?
Makoto:	Um, this is Mr. Kinoshita in room two oh seven. I'm sorry, but I have a problem.
Clerk:	Yes? Is it your room?
Makoto:	No, it's not the room. I've lost something.
Clerk:	Oh, dear. What is it?
Makoto:	Er, well, it's my credit card.
Clerk:	Oh, that's serious. Have you lost anything else? Cash? Traveler's checks?
Makoto:	No, not traveler's checks. I don't have any. But it's my credit card. It's gone!
Clerk:	I hope it wasn't taken from your room!
Makoto:	Well, I'm not sure. But I had it this morning.
Clerk:	Well, I'll put you through to Security.
Makoto:	Oh, thank you. I'm sorry.
Clerk:	It's no problem. Just a moment, please.

Conversation

Listen and check your answers.

Receptionist:	Can I help you?
Makoto:	Yes, please. My camera is missing.
Receptionist:	I see. Where did you lose it?
Makoto:	Somewhere in the hotel, I think.
Receptionist:	OK. When did you last see it?
Makoto:	Last night.
Receptionist:	Right. What does it look like?
Makoto:	It's small and black.
Receptionist:	I see. Any other details?
Makoto:	Yes. It's a Minolta.
Receptionist:	OK. I'll just check if it's here.

Unit 19 Goodbye and thanks!

Listening

These people are saying goodbye. Listen. Circle T (true) or F (false).

Conversation 1: Miki

Amy:	Hello.
Miki:	Hi, Amy. It's me, Miki.
Amy:	Hi, Miki, how are you doing?
Miki:	Fine. But Rie and I are leaving the States tomorrow. I called to say goodbye.
Amy:	Oh, it was great to see you again, Miki.
Miki:	And you. Thanks for looking after us so well in New York. We had a wonderful time.
Amy:	I enjoyed it, too.
Miki:	You must come over to Japan some time and visit us. We can show you around.
Amy:	I'd love to. Maybe next year.

Miki:	You're welcome any time. Anyway, bye for now and thanks again!
Amy:	Bye! Take care! Have a good trip!

Conversation 2: Makoto and Mayumi

John:	Oh, I hate saying goodbye!
Mayumi:	Me, too.
John:	It's been really wonderful seeing you.
Makoto:	And we've enjoyed it a lot, too.
John:	Yes, well I've really enjoyed it. And I've got a small gift for you.
Mayumi:	Oh! Thank you. It's a painting! Of your house?
John:	Yes, I did it myself.
Mayumi:	Ah, yes … and we have this present for you.
John:	Oh, Mayumi, Makoto! You shouldn't have.
Makoto:	They're Japanese rice crackers.
John:	Oh, that's really, really nice.(*tears all round*)

Conversation 3: Kazuo

Man:	Well, so long, Kazuo. It's been great meeting you again.
Woman:	Are you ready? Have you got all your suitcases and things? I don't want you to forget anything.
Kazuo:	Oh, I've got everything, I think. I'm going back with a lot of things! Thank you for the lovely presents.
Woman:	Oh, and thanks for yours. We'll look at them and think of you.
Kazuo:	And thank you for helping me with my English.
Man:	We ought to learn some Japanese, I guess.
Kazuo:	Yes. (*laughs*)
Man:	We'd love to see you when you visit England again.
Kazuo:	Er, yes. I think it won't be for a long time, though!
Woman:	Oh, well. Come on. Time to go. We don't want you to miss your plane.

Conversation 4: Sanae

Woman:	The time has gone so quickly, Sanae.
Sanae:	I know. Thank you for everything.
Man:	We should thank you. You've been a great guest.
Sanae:	I've really enjoyed myself.
Woman:	The dog's going to miss you too. (*sound of dog barking*)
Sanae:	Oh I'd like to take him to Japan.
Woman:	ou know, at the beginning, I didn't think you liked American food. It's very different from Japanese food.
Sanae:	Oh, no, no! I really enjoyed it. It was great.
Woman:	Oh, good.
Man:	Now, I think we should get going.

Conversation 5: Jun

Boy:	When are you leaving, Jun?
Jun:	Oh, in a few minutes, I think.
Girl:	Can I go to Japan, Mom?
Woman:	One day, dear, but not now.
Man:	So, are you ready, Jun?
Woman:	Well, it's goodbye. For now, anyway. It's been wonderful.
Jun:	And thank you again for everything.

Woman:	You're welcome.
Man:	The car's ready! Hurry up!
Woman:	Now, remember. You're welcome to come stay with us anytime. Why don't you come for Christmas?
Jun:	I'd love that.
Boy and Girl:	Christmas! Christmas! That's great.
All:	Bye. Goodbye. See you again. See you at Christmas, we hope.(*sound of car driving away*)

Conversation

Listen and check your answers.

Mr. Todd:	Well, it's time to say goodbye.
Koji:	Yes. I'm going to miss you all.
Mr. Todd:	We enjoyed having you stay.
Koji:	Please say goodbye to Sam for me.
Mr. Todd:	Of course I will.
Koji:	You know, at first I thought I'd be homesick, but it wasn't a problem at all.
Mr. Todd:	Well, we're glad you had a good time.
Koji:	This is for you. It's from Japan.
Mr. Todd:	Oh, you shouldn't have!
Koji:	It's a paper lantern.
Mr. Todd:	That's very kind of you. Thank you very much.
Koji:	Well, thank you again. Goodbye!
Mr. Todd:	Goodbye. Have a safe trip.

Unit 20   How many bags do you have?

Listening

These people are checking in for their flights. Listen. Check the correct answer.

Conversation 1: Koji

Clerk:	Smoking or non-smoking?
Koji:	Non-smoking, please.
Clerk:	And where would you like to sit?
Koji:	Er, sorry. I don't understand.
Clerk:	Your seat. Would you like a window seat? An aisle seat?
Koji:	Oh, I see. Er, window, please.
Clerk:	Window?
Koji:	Er, no, aisle, please. I'd like an aisle seat, please. Sorry.
Clerk:	No problem. Now, do you have any bags to check in?

Conversation 2: Koji

Clerk:	Here you are, sir. Here's your boarding pass and your baggage receipts.
Koji:	Thank you.
Clerk:	Your flight is on time. Please go to gate eighteen when your flight is called.
Koji:	I'm sorry, could you repeat that, please?
Clerk:	Yes. Please go to gate eighteen when the flight is called.
Koji:	Eighty?
Clerk:	No, eighteen, one eight.
Koji:	Oh, I see. Thank you.

Conversation 3: Miki

Miki:	Excuse me?
Clerk:	Good morning. How may I help you?
Miki:	I want to check in, please.
Clerk:	Which flight are you on?
Miki:	Oh, Delta. DL, um, one eight one six.
Clerk:	One eight one six? Are you sure? Er, may I see your ticket, please?
Miki:	Oh, yes. Here you are.
Clerk:	Yes, miss. Your flight is DL one six one eight.
Miki:	Oh, thanks. Can I check in here?
Clerk:	No. You need to go over there.
Miki:	Oh, OK. Thanks.

Conversation 4: Miki

Clerk:	Do you have any bags to check?
Miki:	Ah, yes. These two.
Clerk:	Two suitcases?
Miki:	Two. Yes.
Clerk:	OK. Would you put them on the scales, please?
Miki:	Sorry? I didn't understand.
Clerk:	I need to weigh your luggage. Could you put them here, please?
Miki:	Oh, I see.
Clerk:	OK. That's fine. Do you have any carry-on luggage?
Miki:	Um, yes, here.
Clerk:	Oh, I see. I'm afraid you can only have one piece of carry-on luggage. You seem to have, er, three.
Miki:	Yes, three.
Clerk:	I'm sorry, but you can only take one piece onto the plane. You'll have to check two of them.

Conversation

Listen to this conversation between Rie and a check-in clerk. Fill in the blanks.

Rie:	Can I check in here for flight DL one six one eight?
Clerk:	Yes, you can. May I see your ticket and passport, please?
Rie:	Yes. Here you are.
Clerk:	Would you like smoking or non-smoking?
Rie:	Non-smoking, please.
Clerk:	Fine. Now, would you like a window seat?
Rie:	Er, yes, please.
Clerk:	OK. Do you have any bags to check?
Rie:	Yes, I have two suitcases.
Clerk:	Could you put them on the scales, please?
Rie:	Sure.
Clerk:	Did you pack these bags yourself?
Rie:	Yes, I did.
Clerk:	That's fine. Here's your boarding pass. Please go to gate sixteen when the flight is called.
Rie:	I see. Thank you.
Clerk:	Have a good flight!